Jewels by Cartier

White sidewall tires available at extra cost.

IT IS A HAPPY experience for a Cadillac dealer when he delivers a car into the hands of an owner who is moving up to Cadillac for the first time. For, in most cases, it means the fulfillment of a long-cherished hope. There are a few indeed who are not aware that the person who sits behind the wheel of a Cadillac is enjoying many advantages, which Cadillac alone provides. And it is only natural to wish for the best. This great preference for Cadillac goes on an on, year after year—without any relationship to a current model or to any particular series of cars. It is rooted, rather, in Cadillac's past—and in the great promise that this past implies for the future. During almost half a century, Cadillac cars have been built to the most inflexible standards of automotive goodness—and it is obvious that to these standards they will continue to be built. If you are among the many who are tired of compromise with any of the basic motor car virtues—we invite you to go visit your Cadillac dealer. He considers it a special privilege to welcome new owners into the Cadillac group.

★ CADILLAC MOTOR CAR DIVISION ★ GENERAL MOTORS CORPORATION ★

Statistics

	1950	1960
Population of the United States	151.3 million	179.3 million
Number of states in the United States	48	50
Population by race:		
White	135.1 million	158.8 million
Other	16.2 million	20.5 million
Population by sex:		
Male	75.2 million	88.3 million
Female	76.1 million	91 million
Population per square mile	42.6	50.6
Life expectancy:		
Male	65.6	66.6
Female	71.1	73.1
Three leading causes of death	Heart disease Cancer Influenza/Pneumonia	Heart disease Cancer Influenza/Pneumonia
Homicides	7,942	8,464
Suicides	17,145	19,041
Prison population	166,123	212,957
Prisoners executed	82	56
Unemployment rate	5.3%	5.5%
Average annual employee earnings	$2,992	$4,743
Number of business failures	9,162	15,445
Number of stock and bond salespeople	11,000	29,000
Number of physicians and surgeons	195,000	230,000
Number of actors and actresses	20,000	18,000
Number of bowlers	1.9 million	5.3 million
Number of golfers	3.2 million	4.4 million
Illiteracy rate	3.2%	2.2%
Percentage of high school graduates	17.6%	23.1%
U.S. passports issued	300,000	853,000
Air fatalities	96	326
Prices:		
dozen eggs	72¢	58¢
quart of milk	21¢	26¢
loaf of bread	14¢	20¢
pound of butter	60¢	75¢
pound of coffee	55¢	75¢
dozen oranges	52¢	75¢

Fearon's OUR CENTURY™

Our Century is a trademark of David S. Lake Publishers. *Our Century 1950–1960.* Copyright © 1989 by David S. Lake Publishers, 500 Harbor Boulevard, Belmont, California 94002. All rights reserved. No part of this publication may be reproduced by any means, transmitted, or translated into a machine language without written permission from the publisher.

ISBN 0–8224–5081–X

1. 9 8 7 6 5 4 3 2 1

Writer: S. D. Jones
Designer: Detta Penna

Photographs: Cover (Elvis Presley, Albert Schweitzer) and pp. 4, 30, 47: UPI/Bettmann Archive; Cover (Mr. and Mrs. Eisenhower, Mr. and Mrs. Nixon, Fidel Castro) and pp. 5–9, 15, 16, 20, 24, 25, 27, 31, 37–40, 43–46, 48–53, 55–57, 60–62, 64: UPI/Bettmann Newsphotos; Cover (Anthony Eden, Winston Churchill, Abdul Nasser, Queen Elizabeth II, GI sitting in the snow) and pp. 10–14, 17–19, 21–23, 28, 29, 32–35, 41, 42, 53, 54, 58, 59, 61, 63: The Bettmann Archive; pp. 57, 59: Springer/Bettmann Film Archive. Advertisements on endpapers, photo p. 5: The D'Arcy Collection, University of Illinois at Urbana-Champaign.

1950-1960

The latest in drive-in diners: orders are sent from the kitchen directly to the customers in their cars. The trays move along a "track," and then return the same way.

Transportation

America Has a Love Affair With the Automobile

The American passion for wheels reached its peak in the fifties. All across the country people were taking to the road. Being on the move was what mattered. Where they were going was not so important as how they got there.

For the first time in years Americans had time on their hands

and money to spend. So they added a new element to the American dream—the status symbol. And no other status symbol packed a bigger punch than the automobile.

The car of the fifties was big, powerful, and solid. No longer was a car just a means of transportation. It was freedom and luxury on wheels.

Having a simple car to get you to the store and back was not enough. Now driving had to be fun . . . and as easy as possible. Phrases like, "Dyna Flow," "Power Flight," and "Merc-O-Matic" spoke of the power waiting at your fingertips.

Adjectives like "DeLuxe," "Custom," "Royal" and "Super Jet"

brought images of glamour and prestige to mind. Huge tailfins were said to "add stability at high speeds." Wrap around windshields increased visibility. Huge torpedo-like growths on the front bumpers were . . . well, they didn't really do anything, but they looked great. Some new cars looked like rockets.

The cars of the fifties were getting a little safer, too. Seat belts were introduced as extras. All-steel construction made cars stronger, and engines and transmissions were becoming more efficient.

The car population was growing faster than the highway system.

Prices varied. A new 1958 Dodge, with push button automatic transmission, cost about $2,500. But a 1958 El Dorado Brougham, from Cadillac, retailed for $13,074.

"Freedom" for Teenagers

The impact of the automobile went beyond leisure time. It changed Americans' entire way of life. Cars with names like "Nomad," "Ranger," "Rambler," and "Cruiser," carried people all across America. The country was shrinking. People no longer had to stay in the same town where they grew up. They could see different cities and towns with ease. Now people didn't have to *live* in the city to *work* in the city. The new ease of travel gave rise to the development of suburbs.

Teenagers, too, found new freedom. They were no longer forced to steal kisses on the front porch swing. They could get out of the house in dad's "Rebel" or "Dragon." A new youth culture was created around the car. Drive-in movies and diners became popular. During the fifties, kids started spending less time with family and more time with friends.

For housewives, shopping and running errands took a new twist. Mom was no longer tied to the house, though she often became the family driver. She might drop her husband off at the train station, then drive the kids to school and later pick them up. In between, she drove to the market and the cleaners. Finally, she picked her husband up after work. In one short decade, her headquarters moved from the kitchen to the car.

But America's love affair with the automobile was a rocky one. In 1955, sales reached a record 6.5 million cars. There were 50 million car registrations. But the car population was growing faster than the highway system. Drivers worried about highway congestion and exhaust pollution.

Their fears did not stop them from buying, though. By the end of the decade, the car was no longer a status symbol—it was a necessity. ∎

Drive-in movies did big business during the decade. Here a couple of "lovebirds" enjoy a band concert at the theater. When the sun goes down, the movie screen will light up.

The Chrysler Imperial was one of the more popular luxury cars of the fifties.

Civil Defense Strengthened

Americans Take Steps to Survive H-Bomb Attack

"H–Bomb Can Wipe Out Any City," the headlines read. "The United States can now build a Hydrogen bomb big enough to destroy any city."

The news was shocking. It ushered in the Hydrogen Age. No longer would a bomb's power be measured in thousands of tons, but in "megatons." Megatons are *millions* of tons of TNT.

Of course, most people already knew what an atomic bomb could do. The A-bomb was dropped on Hiroshima and Nagasaki at the end of World War II. It caused horrible loss of life and property.

But that was different. Dropping the A-bomb was a desperate act for a desperate situation. The result was the *end* of conflict. But the next war,

the generals said, would *start* with such a bomb.

On March 26, 1953, an H-bomb was exploded with a force almost 700 times greater than the bombs dropped on Japan. It was part of a test run by the U.S. military. The experts said it could destroy all life within a 50-mile radius of New York City.

The thought of such power was frightening enough. But what if the testing of such bombs went out of control? The army assured Americans that was not possible. But what about the enemy? Surely the Russians must have such a weapon, too.

For years, Americans had heard all about Russian spies. Senator Joseph McCarthy and Vice-President Richard Nixon had charged that

Communists were at every level of our government. In Korea, hadn't Eisenhower threatened the Reds with an atomic bomb? Surely the Reds would use it on America if they wanted to!

With all the cold war threats being hurled back and forth, the idea of atomic war was very real. No one escaped the fear of the bomb that was gripping middle-class America. Even the movies were no escape. Films like *On the Beach* and *The Day the World Ended* gave people a nightmare vision. These films imagined the possibility of the end of the world through atomic warfare.

Science fiction films were very popular, too. *Invasion* was the general theme of those films. Perhaps it was Martians invading the earth.

Third-grade pupils in Cleveland, Ohio, practice an air-raid drill. Drills such as these were held in thousands of schools across the country in the fifties.

Or maybe violent and ugly creatures taking over the suburbs. In either case, no one was safe. These films reflected a fearful state of mind. Americans felt exposed and helpless.

Underground Protection

The bomb shelter gave Americans a chance to fight back. Building a bomb shelter was a way for sane people to protect themselves from a crazy situation. "We can't stop the bombs," they seemed to say. "But we can save our families." And so suburban Americans dug in for the long war.

Backyards were dug up. Swing sets were moved. Swimming pools were covered over. The bomb shelter became a common sight in cities throughout the country.

Some families spent entire weekends practicing underground survival.

If a shelter was built in cooperation with the civil defense program, 100% financing was available. The typical shelter was stocked with necessities like canned food and water, a first aid kit, a chemical toilet, cots, an air blower, gas masks, a generator, a flashlight, and tools.

But owning your own shelter was only part of the answer. You also had to be able to get to the shelter and survive in there during an attack. So families practiced.

Well-meaning parents would wake their kids up at all hours of the night. Like drill sergeants, they barked out orders. A successful drill required speed and organization. Some families even spent entire weekends practicing underground survival while less-concerned neighbors barbecued.

Civil defense became a concern away from home, too. After all, a bomb attack could come at any time—day or night. Air-raid drills were held in schools throughout America.

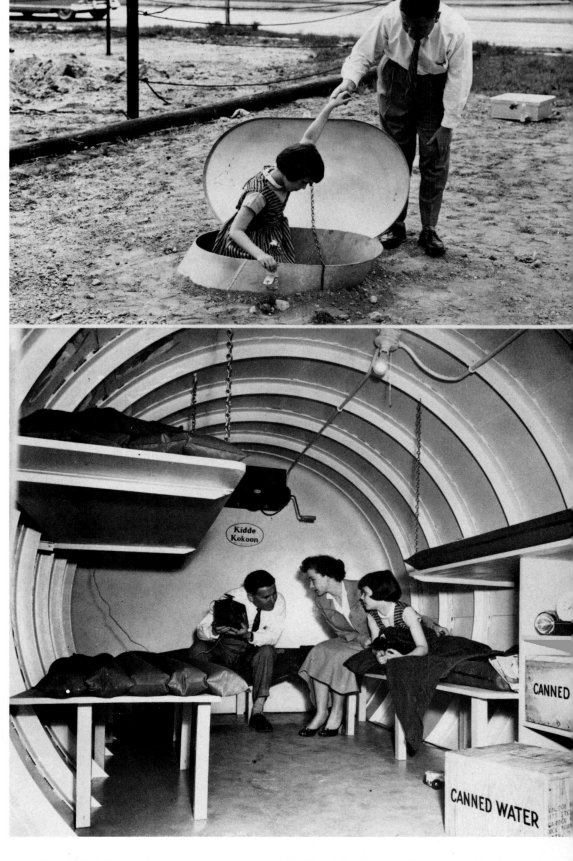

School children learned to recognize the sound of the air-raid siren. That shriek meant you should drop from your chair and crunch under your desk—head down between knees, hands over head.

As the decade ended, some Americans guessed that their bomb shelters might become a joke to their less fearful neighbors. But the threat of worldwide destruction was no joke to anyone. ∎

Thousands of Americans installed bomb shelters, such as this one, in their backyards during the fifties. This shelter, located ten feet underground is equipped with five bunks and air mattresses. It also contains a fan which draws air that has been "purified" through a special filter.

Fads in the Fifties

It Was Real Cool, Man . . . You Dig?

Communists, it seemed, were everywhere—hiding under every bed and peeking through every keyhole. The threat of atomic destruction loomed over every head. The Cold War was creating terrible tension, and people needed a break from it all.

Many Americans coped with the tension of the times by indulging in a wide array of fads. The fads of the fifties were usually wacky, and central to any fad—short lived.

A new generation of kids was growing up. They had time on their hands and their parents were giving them pocket money to spend. So young people, especially, went from one fad to another.

Davy Crockett, "King of the Wild Frontier," was one of the biggest fads. The real American hero may have been "born on a mountain top in Tennessee," but his fame reached all over the United States 120 years after his death at the Alamo.

"Davy Crockett" was a Disney TV show which aired in the mid-fifties. Fess Parker played the brave frontiersman. His appeal was instant. Soon kids everywhere were sporting "coonskin" caps and Davy T-shirts. The Davy Crockett theme song sold more than four million records.

People may have looked silly wearing the furry hats, but they looked even more bizarre wearing 3D glasses. This fad began with a movie called *Bwana Devil* in 1952.

TV star Garry Moore and four great-great-great-great-grandchildren of Davy Crockett pose with the headwear Crockett made famous: the coonskin cap.

8

But it wasn't long before dozens of science fiction and horror movies were being made in 3D.

The 3D glasses change the typical, flat, two-dimensional image on the screen. They make the image appear three dimensional. Lions, spears, vampires, and Martian death-rays all seem to leap from the screen toward the viewer's seat.

Many Americans didn't have to go to the movies to see Martians. Martians seemed to be showing up everywhere. An amazing number of people reported seeing flying saucers and other UFOs. Dozens of amateur photographers snapped pictures of them. Odd banana-shaped missiles, saucers, and glowing objects were shown lighting up the night skies.

Where were these space invaders coming from? Were they friendly? What did the American government know about them? The Air Force claimed ignorance. But people figured they must know something. Hundreds of sightings were made every year. Private studies were made. Even the Air Force spent tens of thousands of dollars on their own study. But after all the research, no one had learned a thing about UFOs.

Language—Twists and Turns

But they did know a thing or two about Hula-Hoops. Hula-Hoops were plastic tubes formed into large rings. In 1958 millions of kids twirled them around their waists, arms, necks, and heads. Schools and clubs sponsored Hula-Hoop contests. One winner kept his hoop up for 3,000 spins.

He must have felt pretty "cool" about that. Some of his pals probably would have said he was "far out." But when Mom and Dad told him to stop twirling and start doing homework, he probably would have thought they were "square."

The English language spun around faster than a Hula-Hoop. In the fifties, each group had its own fad lingo. Even advertising men had a language all their own. When they wanted to know what the public

thought about something, they'd "run it up the flagpole." They didn't just think up ideas, they "pressure cooked" or "kicked around" ideas. But for kids, the admen were just plain L7—that means "square" to all you "cats" who aren't "hip."

After a hard day of spotting UFOs and spinning Hula-Hoops, young people needed a rest. When nothing else was "shaking," students could be seen cramming. No, not studying. They crammed into phone booths, cars, and dorm rooms. In short, anything that was too small to comfortably fit dozens of students. That was just one more fifties fad. Do you dig it, man? ∎

You think the *movie* is funny—just look around you. 3D glasses were the rage for a while with fifties' movie audiences. Americans loved to see science fiction and horror films spring to life. The movies cost a few dollars. The headaches were free.

Hula-Hoops were a big fad during the fifties. Not everyone caught the hang of it.

The smaller the waist, the fuller the skirt, the better the look. In this popular dress style of the fifties, the figure-molding bodice stands in sharp contrast to the wide skirt which is supported by a stiff petticoat.

After dark, elegant women of the fifties wore form-fitting "cocktail dresses" like this one of soft silk crepe. Gloves and a smart evening hat completed the "picture perfect" image.

Fashion

From "A" to "Y"—A Constant Change of Styles

The fashion industry boomed in the fifties. Fads were popular in every walk of life, and fashion was no exception. Each year brought a new list of "in" and "out" clothing.

The "A" look, "H" look, and "Y" look were fashion terms used by the French fashion designer Dior. They were typical of the dizzying number of style changes that occurred during the decade.

Skirts flared out at an odd, almost sharp angle. Or they hugged the legs and dropped straight down. Or they were simply a single tube of cotton.

Shorts might be very short, like "short-shorts," or long, like Bermuda shorts. Polka dots and the color pink seemed to be everywhere. And a more revealing "two piece" bathing suit made its debut.

For women, hair was typically cut short. Many permed their hair into a "poodle" style, setting it close to the scalp in curly ringlets. Others sported the "Italian look," a short-cropped boyish cut.

For men, hair was either very short, as in the flattop or crew-cut look, or it was long. To get the duck-tail look the hair was dampened, oiled, and swept back to a kind of, well . . . duck tail.

The gray flannel suit was a big hit in the fifties. A whole army of men now belonged to the new group of postwar office workers. Dubbed "Organization Men," they dressed in somber colors and wore "sincere" ties. Most men still wore hats to work every day.

For kids the choices were even greater—though they usually wound up wearing the same things kids usually do. Chinos, tan cotton trousers, were a hot ticket. Varsity letter sweaters were big with the athletic crowd. And in shoes, loafers or "sneaks" were a must. Blue jeans, once the uniform of the farm boy, became the uniform of both the "hip" and the "hood." And speaking of bad boys, black leather was in for rebels. For the "Beat" crowd, black, in general, was the groovy color.

Glasses were pretty square. If you wore them, you might hear cries of "four eyes" or "nerd" (unless you were wearing that letter sweater). ■

The War That Nobody Won

Korea. It was supposed to be a short-term "police action." But it turned into a long and bitter war. Peace talks seemed to go on continuously. So did the fighting. Between the war's beginning in 1950 and its end in 1953, millions of civilians were hurt or killed. And some of the problems that existed before the war are still not resolved.

After World War II, the United States and Russia decided to split Korea into two sections. The purpose was to help organize the surrender of the Japanese who had controlled Korea for more than 30 years. The northern half would be under Communist control. The southern half would be under the eye of the United States.

The two powers drew an imaginary line through the country to split it up. They called this line the "38th parallel." It ran from the east coast to the west coast through the city of Panmunjom.

But the governments of both the North and South claimed to have power over the whole country. So even before the war, the two sides were enemies. Every now and then fighting would spring up. Early in 1950 there were battles all along the 38th parallel.

The South Koreans had warned their U.S. allies that the North was planning to invade the South. They knew that the Communists in the North wanted to unite all of Korea under one government. And they wanted to do it *by force*. But the United States didn't listen to the warnings.

The United States had taken its soldiers out of Korea in 1949. The troubles in Korea were not considered that important to America.

Most U.S. military leaders thought the next war would be another *worldwide* war.

They did not expect a conventional war, one fought with lots of manpower and ordinary weapons. The world seemed instead to be moving toward atomic war. After all, an atomic bomb had changed the course of the last war. In another conflict it seemed logical to expect more atomic bombs. But that did not happen.

On June 23, 1950, the Soviet-backed North Korean troops invaded the South.

For the next three years the United States and South Korean ⇨

U.S. forces in Korea were faced with harsh winter battles during the three-year war.

American and South Korean forces capture North Koreans at Inchon in September 1950. Prisoner resettlement was a major sticking point during the drawn-out peace talks.

forces fought the North. Every time U.S. forces gained ground, they were beaten back. Every time peace seemed close at hand, more fighting broke out. It was maddening and frustrating for U.S. military leaders.

Many of the U.S. soldiers who fought in Korea had also fought in World War II. They were tired of fighting. Many of them also did not understand exactly why they were there. All they knew was that the South Koreans needed help. Communist forces had surprised them by capturing Seoul, the capital, and marching deep into the South.

At the time of the invasion President Truman had sent military advisers—but no troops. He told General Douglas MacArthur to send U.S. arms from Japan to help the South Koreans. Before long however, Truman wound up sending U.S. troops to aid them.

Normally, the president has to get approval from Congress to involve U.S. forces in a foreign war. But Truman did not have to do this in Korea. The reason for this was complex. What it came down to was

Every time peace seemed close at hand, more fighting broke out.

that the United States became involved through the workings of the United Nations.

For weeks, the UN Security Council had been talking about the problems in Korea. They ordered the North Koreans back behind the 38th parallel, but the North Koreans would not obey. Also, the Soviet member of the UN Security Council did not show up for meeting after meeting.

MacArthur in Command

The world community feared the North Koreans were planning a full-scale attack. Many member nations were angry that the Soviets were skipping important UN meetings. They called for all member nations to help out with any assistance. For the United States, this "assistance" meant armed soldiers.

By the end of June 1950, President Truman had ordered U.S. troops into Korea to help the South. Most of America's allies also sent in troops to fight the Communists. With approval from the UN Security Council, Truman put Douglas MacArthur in charge of all these international troops. They were all part of the United Nations Command.

By July, Communists were already deep inside South Korea. So the UN troops had their work cut out for them. Their main goal was to protect the city of Pusan, a port in southeastern Korea. The North Koreans were advancing toward Pusan, crushing everything in their path. The U.S. defense was not strong enough to hold them back.

The North Koreans got to within 50 miles of Pusan. Then Lt. General Walton Walker and the U.S. Eighth Army dug in and fought back. They got help from UN fighter planes. Pusan remained safe.

But things didn't look good for the South Koreans. The Communists had made deep advances. The U.S. troops were not giving up any more ground. But they were not *taking* any either.

In order to break this stalemate, General MacArthur made a bold move. On September 15, 1950, he sent U.S. troops ashore at Inchon—almost 200 miles *behind* enemy lines. If the plan did not work, the Marines could have been nearly wiped out. If

it did work, the Communist troops would be trapped. They would be caught between two sets of U.S. forces: the Marines in the North, and the Eighth Army in the South.

The plan worked. The North Korean army began to fall apart. But the joy of victory did not last long. The Truman administration decided to push farther. And MacArthur wanted more victories. ∎

U.S. paratroopers land in Korea to help stop the North Korean surge into South Korean territory.

MacArthur Dismissed From Command

Red China Enters the Korean Conflict

U.S. Marines were stunned by the attack of the Red Chinese Army. Here the Americans begin their long retreat south through subzero temperatures and icy roads in late November 1950.

The original objective of the U.S. forces had been to get the North Koreans out of the South. The United States did that. But instead of settling for that goal, Truman made the same kind of move the North had made. He decided to unite all of Korea under one government—by force. After all, the UN had always wanted that. Now seemed the time to make it happen.

In October the UN voted to make sure that Korea was unified under one democratic government. So MacArthur stayed in the North. In fact, Truman told him to keep pushing North—beyond the 38th parallel. U.S. troops made it all the way to the Yalu river—the border between Korea and Red China.

But once again, the United States did not listen to warnings.

America had been warned that China might enter the war if U.S. troops came too close to its border. Truman worried about this. He had wanted to keep the fighting local—just in Korea. If China were to get involved, he thought, it might open the war up. MacArthur assured him that the Chinese would not attack.

A drive to end the war was on. MacArthur only had to secure the northern borders to make the unification of Korea complete.

But he was surprised. The Chinese did attack. Tens of thousands of soldiers of the "Chinese People's Volunteers" were ready to push the United States back. The fighting was intense. The Eighth Army almost fell apart. The Marines were surrounded. Casualties were high. During the harsh, cold winter of 1950–51, the United States began a long retreat.

> MacArthur's plan was the "wrong war, at the wrong place, at the wrong time, with the wrong enemy."

As the United States, UN, and South Korean troops fell back, the North Koreans and Chinese pushed forward. Soon, the United States was back where it had started—at the 38th parallel. And tension was higher than ever before. So much had been gained and lost in the course of a few months.

The Chinese offensive had surprised and frightened much of the free world. Would this mean that Communist forces would try other aggression? Was Europe safe?

One thing was certain. Korea would never be united by force. The North had tried it and failed. The South had tried it and failed. Unity would only happen through peace.

Everything seemed fine when President Truman met General Douglas MacArthur for the first time in October 1950. Six months later, Truman fired MacArthur when the two argued over war strategy.

But MacArthur had other ideas. He asked the president to let him attack Manchuria, an area in China. Manchuria housed many air bases. It was economically important to China. When Truman said no, MacArthur began making public statements that showed he clearly disagreed with the president. Truman was furious.

And Truman was not the only one to disagree with MacArthur's plans for the war. Another general claimed that the United States should not get too involved in the Far East. He said that MacArthur's plan was, "the wrong war, at the wrong place, at the wrong time, with the wrong enemy."

MacArthur was unconvinced. He continued to disagree publicly with White House policy on the war. Finally, Truman had enough. On April 11, 1951, he fired MacArthur and replaced him with General Matthew Ridgway. ∎

After Many Tries, Peace Comes to Korea

In the months that followed, the fighting went back and forth from north to south of the 38th parallel. Peace negotiations began in July 1951. Both sides spoke less and less about a unified Korea. They seemed willing to accept a divided Korea again. Tens

of thousands of people had already died and neither side had gained anything.

It took weeks just for the two sides to decide what they would talk about! More time passed as the two sides hammered out the details of a truce. Meanwhile, as the politicians talked, the soldiers went on fighting—and dying.

Most tragic was the loss of *civilian* life. The general population

was caught up in the war. The front line of battle seemed to move every day so there were no safe places. Civilians were always on the move. They lived and died on the run, not knowing who to trust.

As many as one million civilians from North and South Korea died during the war.

The question of prisoners was one of the many obstacles to peace. The North said that after the war, it

Surgical teams operate on casualties at the 43d Surgical Hospital in Korea in July 1953.

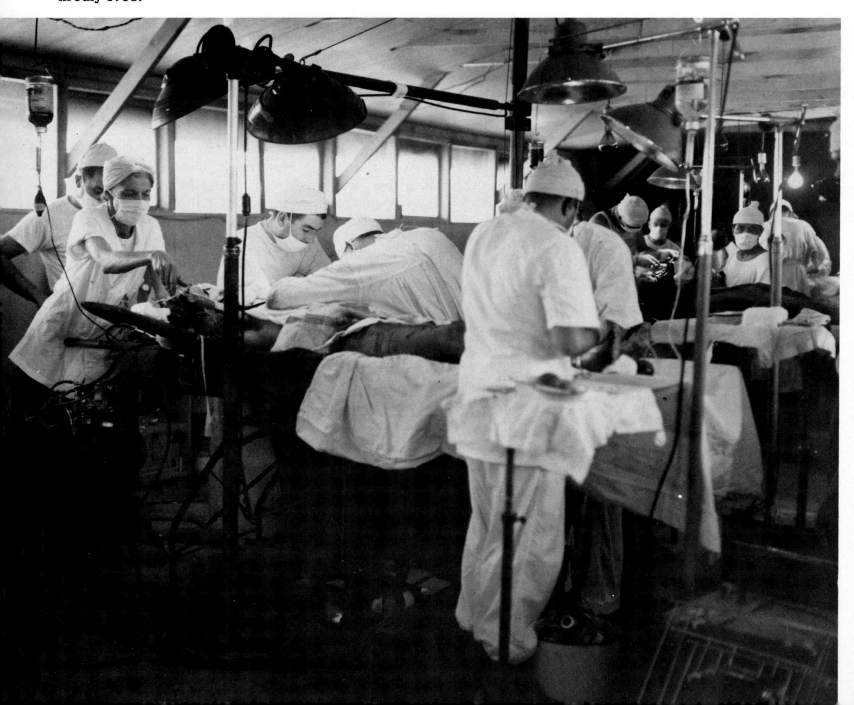

Millions of Korean civilians were killed or left homeless by the constantly advancing and retreating armies.

wanted its prisoners back. The UN Command said that thousands of these prisoners did not *want* to go back. The North said that these prisoners were being forced to say they wanted to stay. They demanded that the prisoners be returned. But the UN Command said no.

Eisenhower Threatens China

The peace talks continued throughout 1952. And the fighting continued as well. But 1952 was an election year in the United States. The Republican candidate, Dwight Eisenhower, said that he would end the war. Americans were tired of the fighting. It did not seem to make any sense. It wasn't like the last war when there was a clear-cut enemy. The whole thing seemed like a nightmare. There was no winner. Only losers.

In December 1952, President-elect Eisenhower made a trip to Korea. He threatened Chinese forces.

He said he might use atomic weapons if they did not agree to a treaty. Before anything was resolved, however, another important thing happened.

As many as one million Korean civilians died during the war.

Josef Stalin, the leader of the Soviet Union, North Korea's strong supporter and China's communist ally, died in March 1953. Tensions between Communists and the United States eased a little with Stalin's death. Both sides were brought back to the bargaining tables. Then on July 27, 1953, a cease-fire was signed.

Both sides claimed a kind of victory, although it wasn't clear how either side won anything. What *was*

clear was that both sides suffered great losses.

The South Koreans lost 58,000 men, and the United States 54,000. Another 275,000 soldiers from both armies were wounded. The Communists had even greater casualties. More than 900,000 Chinese soldiers and more than 500,000 North Korean troops were either killed or wounded.

After all the fighting and killing, things ended pretty much where they had started. When the Geneva Conference was held in 1954, both sides met again to try to iron out their differences. But no one could agree on solutions to the problems of the two Koreas. So the treaty of Panmunjom remained in effect.

Korea was still split in two by the 38th parallel. The North Koreans and South Koreans each had their own governments. Both were still hostile to one another. And there was little hope that Korea would be united any time soon. ■

God Save the Queen

On February 6, 1952, the city of London looked like a ghost town. Movie houses were closed. Lights were dimmed. Almost no one was on the street. The whole country was in mourning because the king had died.

King George VI was only 56 when he died in his sleep. He had been monarch of England for 15 years. Now his eldest daughter, Elizabeth, would become the queen. She was only 25 years old.

When King George died, Elizabeth was in Africa. She and her husband, Prince Philip, were on a five month ceremonial tour of Africa, Australia, and New Zealand.

Described by the papers as "radiantly lovely," Elizabeth took the throne as queen of England on June 2, 1953. She was crowned in Westminster Abbey. Banners of blue and gold hung from the walls. A richly textured rose-colored throne awaited her. Her husband, Prince Philip, traveled with her to Westminster in an ornate gold carriage, driven by a team of horses. The scene was right out of a fairy tale. Some 7,000 invited guests watched the solemn ceremony in the vast hall.

The whole country celebrated her coronation. A quarter of a million people lined the streets, leaning from windows and sitting in trees, hoping to catch a glimpse of their new monarch. Some people without reserved seats waited for days to claim a tiny patch of grass along the street curb.

Elizabeth was the first queen since Victoria (who died in 1901) to wear the royal crown. It had been 115 years since the words, "God save the queen" were heard at a coronation.

Elizabeth's three-year-old son, Prince Charles, became the Prince of Wales. As the next heir in line, he will someday become king of England.

The coronation of the beautiful new queen marked the dawn of a new Elizabethan Age for England. And the joy felt by the British people helped ease their sadness at the loss of their king. ■

The young Queen Elizabeth II smiles for the crowd as she rides home from her coronation at Westminster Abbey in June 1953.

Josef Stalin's death created a great power struggle between Georgi Malenkov (left of coffin) and Nikita Khrushchev (second right from coffin).

Soviet Union Power Struggle

The Aftermath of a Tyrant's Rule

For many people, the name Josef Stalin still causes feelings of fear and hatred. Stalin ruled the Soviet Union from 1929 to 1953. He made the Soviet Union one of the world's great powers. His leadership helped beat back the Nazi armies in World War II. But he was also a tyrant.

Stalin used secret police to terrorize his people into submission. Millions were arrested for minor reasons—usually for having non-conformist attitudes. These people were often sent to concentration camps. Millions died in these camps, or were killed by secret police and the military.

Stalin also created feelings of distrust for Western ways in his people. Everyone was afraid to challenge Stalin's opinions. So the Soviet Union as a whole took a hard line against the West.

When Stalin died in 1953, people in and out of Russia waited to see what would happen next. Soon Stalin's name and approach to governing were being dragged through the mud. A new and different leader was called for. But who would that leader be? Russia was caught up in a power struggle that lasted for years.

There were two powerful people in line to take Stalin's place—Georgi Malenkov and Nikita Khrushchev. Both men wanted to gain power. They knew the mood of the country was anti-Stalin. In order to win support, both tried to distance themselves from the tyrant's tactics.

Each man had a different way to bring about change. Malenkov wanted to push for expansion of industry. Khrushchev wanted to reform and upgrade agriculture.

After Stalin's death, Malenkov was made premier. He tried things his way, but his way failed. Malenkov was forced to resign his post. He had to apologize for his failures. He was demoted. Meanwhile, Khrushchev gained more influence and more power.

Khrushchev in Charge

Marshal Nikolai Bulganin was named to replace Malenkov. But it soon became clear that he was not the man in charge. Khrushchev was.

In fact, through his post as party first secretary, Khrushchev had hand-picked Bulganin to succeed Malenkov.

Khrushchev was able to put younger men in power who would go along with the things he wanted to accomplish. The secret Soviet government began to open up.

For one thing, citizens were allowed inside the Kremlin—the seat

---

Great uprisings in Soviet-controlled countries weakened Khrushchev's grip.

---

of the Russian government. For another, Khrushchev and Premier Bulganin made trips all over Russia. They talked to the people. They learned firsthand what ordinary people wanted. Greater freedom was allowed within Russia. The power of the secret police—so fearsome in Stalin's time—was weakening. ⇨

But as Khrushchev pushed for greater reforms, the conservatives in government pushed back. Khrushchev found himself caught between two groups—the government conservatives on the one hand, and a people longing for reform on the other.

Great uprisings in Soviet-controlled countries weakened Khrushchev's grip. People in Hungary and Poland demanded more and more changes. In 1957, the conservatives in the ruling Soviet Presidium voted to oust him.

But Khrushchev outmaneuvered them. He said the Presidium vote did not count until it was approved by the entire Central Committee of the party. And he was right. The trouble was, committee members who were most loyal to him were not nearby to vote. So Khrushchev had his supporters flown in from the farthest corners of Russia to vote for him. The Presidium vote was overturned and the conservatives lost. Khrushchev's most vocal challengers were demoted and sent away to distant places.

Finally, Khrushchev gained complete control of the Soviet government. In 1958 he ousted Bulganin and made himself premier as well as first secretary of the Communist party. After five years, the great power struggle was over—and Khrushchev had won. ∎

Nikita Khrushchev won a five-year power struggle to gain control of the Soviet Union.

King Farouk I was king of Egypt from 1936 to 1952. He was a weak ruler whose government was marred by widespread corruption.

Suez Canal Crisis

A Bitter Struggle for a Crucial Waterway

All eyes were on the Middle East in November of 1956. For three weeks, people all over the world worried over the events occurring along a small strip of water called the Suez Canal.

A war was taking place there. It wasn't a giant war. Other problems might have seemed more important. But everyone was afraid because this little war could easily turn into a bigger one. The stakes were high. Threats of nuclear war were made. It was a tense time for the whole world.

The trouble in that part of the world began years earlier. It started with King Farouk I of Egypt. Farouk was Egypt's king from 1936 to 1952. Generally, he was not a skillful ruler. He did not have a strong enough hand to control his people. Many of

the officials closest to him were very corrupt.

Eventually Farouk lost support within his army. Then internal rivalries began to arise. People competed with each other to get more power within the government. Farouk's government began to unravel.

Then the military turned against him. A man named Gamal Abdel Nasser lead a *coup*—a quick, illegal overthrow—of Farouk's government. This action forced Farouk to give up his throne.

A man named Mohammed Naguib was put in charge as Egypt's new president. Naguib formed a republic. He had many reform ideas. For one thing, he was in favor of a more constitutional style government. But his time as president did

not last long. Nasser, the man who had led the military coup, was a much stronger leader. He was also more popular with the people. He ousted Naguib, and in 1954, made himself Egyptian premier. As the country's new leader, Nasser took on many responsibilities—and many problems as well.

Crucial Oil Supplier

Egypt is a country with a long, rich history. It is also located in one of the most important and sensitive areas of the world. Two-thirds of the world's known oil reserves are in the Middle East. Three-quarters of Europe's oil supply comes from this part of the world. Nations like England, the United States, and ⇨

ize Egypt and make it a great power in the world. And he wanted to make life better for his people. To do this, he got help from both the free world and the Soviet Union.

Nasser wanted to build a dam at a city called Aswan. This dam would help irrigate crops. It would give Egypt the energy it needed to modernize. But the dam would cost millions of dollars. Europe and the United States said they would help pay for it. But they put conditions on the money. They said Nasser would have to cut off his growing ties with the Soviets.

Nasser's Bold Move

Nasser was angry at these conditions. He threatened to go to Russia for the money. In turn, the U.S. government became angry at Nasser. They called off the deal. No money—no dam.

So Nasser came up with another plan to get the money. It was his plan that caused the military crisis in the Suez Canal.

The Suez Canal was "the spinal column of the British Empire."

In July 1956, Nasser "nationalized" the canal. That is, he took the control of the canal away from private businesses. He gave that control back to the state of Egypt. Only a month before, Britain had removed the last of its troops from the canal zone. In doing so, Britain was living up to an agreement signed with Egypt in 1954. Under the terms, Britain would remove all its troops while Egypt guaranteed freedom of canal navigation.

However, "nationalizing" the canal was not Britain's idea of "guaranteeing freedom of canal navigation." Nasser's plan called for using the revenues from the canal to build his Aswan Dam.

Gamal Nasser led the coup that toppled King Farouk.

France need the oil. And they need to ship oil in and out of the area, safely and quickly. Their ships use the Suez Canal to take the oil out. And for England, the Suez Canal is also a quick route to India and the East.

The Suez Canal is about 100 miles long. It connects the Mediterranean Sea with the Red Sea. Many ships from different countries use the canal every day. For years the canal was run by private businesses. The French took care of the day-to-day administration of the canal, and the British were responsible for its security.

The British government had a lot at stake in the Suez Canal. They owned part of the business which operated it. Three out of every four ships that used the canal were British. The government had an 80,000 man force permanently stationed in the Canal Zone to protect the "freedom of navigation." As one politician said, the Suez Canal was "the spinal column of the British Empire."

Of course, when Nasser took power, he knew how important Egypt was to the rest of the world. He pushed through many reforms in his country. He wanted to industrial-

British prime minister Anthony Eden, left, with former prime minister Winston Churchill. Eden was responsible for Britain's ill-fated attempt to seize control of the Suez Canal in 1956.

England and France claimed that Nasser could not legally nationalize the canal. They were afraid of Nasser's growing power and popularity. They were afraid of his ties to the Soviets. They feared he could do whatever he wanted with the canal. He had to be stopped.

But Nasser did have the right to take the canal. In a time of crisis many countries have taken over private property for public use. Nasser promised to keep the canal open. But the British and French were not satisfied.

At first they tried to get the United States to help them. But America's interests were not as tied to the canal as those of England and France. It was also an election year in America. The thought of getting into a crisis in the Middle East was not welcomed by anyone in the U.S. government.

France and Britain found themselves alone. They decided to use force to bring Nasser to his knees.

Britain and France allowed Israel to invade Egypt and seize its territories. Here Israeli soldiers round up some prisoners.

And they had a willing partner, Israel, to help them. This was their plan: they asked Israel to attack Egypt. Israel had wanted Egyptian-held land on the Sinai Peninsula anyway. So Israel agreed.

Britain and France knew that Egypt would fight back. Their plan was for British and French troops to swoop into the canal zone. This would force both Egypt and Israel to withdraw. Then, the British and French would *stay* at the canal in order to "save" it from being destroyed. In doing this, Britain and France would get back control of the canal. In addition, Israel would get the land and power it wanted, and Nasser would be taught a lesson.

On October 29, 1956, the plan went into effect. The three countries ganged up on Egypt. But the plan didn't work. Russia helped Egypt with weapons. It even threatened England and France with nuclear war. And still, the United States didn't help. It even condemned Britain's aggression. The United Nations also stepped in. The UN demanded that all parties agree to a cease-fire and that France and Britain get out of the area.

On November 6, the British and French withdrew their forces. The crisis ended. In the eyes of the Egyptian people, Nasser and Egypt had scored a great victory. The canal was still under Egyptian control. ∎

Hungarians Revolt Against Soviet Rule

It began as only a demonstration. Then it turned into a revolt. Finally the revolt became a brief, but bloody war.

The war was waged by Soviet troops and Hungarian secret police against the people of Hungary. In a few short days, during October 1956, 20,000 civilians were killed. About the same number were jailed. As many as 200,000 more people went into exile. The capital city of Budapest lay in ruins.

At stake was control of the Hungarian Communist government. The Soviet Union wanted its own people in power. But the Hungarian people wanted a more democratic style government run by people who were *not* closely tied to Russia.

The Hungarian Communist government had no popular support. But it did have tanks. On the other hand, the Hungarian people had a passion for freedom. But they didn't have any helpful allies.

Relations between the Soviet Union and Hungary had been strained for many years. Hungarians had never felt a deep, historic tie with the Russians. A weak Communist government had come to power in 1919. But the Hungarians had bitterly fought against it. They were so anti-communist that they supported the Nazis against Russia in World War II. Near the end of the war, the

> The Hungarian Communist government had no popular support. But it did have tanks.

Germans turned against their former ally and overthrew the Hungarian government. In 1944 the Red Army advanced and beat the Germans back. In the battle for Hungary, the Hungarian people were terrorized and murdered by *both* the Nazis and the Communists.

After the war, Soviet leader Josef Stalin put his own people in power. Matyas Rakosi became the puppet leader of the Hungarians. His government was repressive and cruel. Anyone who spoke out against

Hungarian freedom fighters, armed to the teeth, fought off Soviet and Hungarian communist forces in November 1956. Tens of thousands of Hungarians were killed or jailed by the Communist troops.

Hungarians smash a statue of the hated Soviet leader, Josef Stalin.

the government was jailed. Many of his political opponents were killed.

The people of Hungary grew tired of Rakosi and of his style of communism. Every Hungarian seemed to know of someone who had been jailed, hurt, or killed. They hated Stalin and Rakosi and what these men stood for.

Then Stalin died in 1953 and a less harsh Soviet leadership took power in Moscow. Rakosi was replaced as premier by a more moderate leader, Imre Nagy. Hungarians no longer felt that they were under the thumb of repression. They complained about the government. They pressed for better conditions at home and at work. Nagy began to make changes to give the people more personal freedom.

But Nagy's reforms were opposed by other Communist officials in the Hungarian government. In 1955 he was replaced as premier by Rakosi. When he returned to his old policies of repression, unrest among the people began to spread.

In mid-1956, Rakosi was replaced once more as leader. But that didn't stop the opposition, because the new leadership continued his policies. The people rallied around their own choice for premier— Imre Nagy. By October, violence had erupted throughout the country. The Communists could not hold onto their shaky, unpopular government.

A Few, Short Days of Freedom

On October 24, the Hungarian people won. Their man Nagy took the leadership post once again. Hungarians went wild with joy. They destroyed paintings and statues of Stalin, the hated symbol of their past. Nagy released thousands of political prisoners. He spoke of breaking away from the Soviet Union and moving toward a neutral international position.

For a few short days, Hungarians experienced unheard of freedom. But these days were also marked by violence. Dozens of Soviet secret police were lynched by the Hungarians. These same secret police had tortured and killed many Hungarians in the past.

This situation frightened the Russians. Other countries under their control had also started talking about reforms. Things could spin out of control. The Hungarians, they decided, had to be stopped.

Just a few days after Nagy was thrust into power, Soviet troops and tanks rolled in. The Russians shelled Budapest. The Hungarian civilians were no match for Soviet armed forces. The uprising was crushed swiftly and completely.

Premier Nagy was taken prisoner. The Russians promised he would go free. But they did not set him free. He was jailed and later executed.

During the revolt, the Hungarians had cried out for help. They asked the United States to save them from destruction. But 1956 was an election year in America. The revolt came just days before the vote. No

The free world had left the Hungarian people stranded.

one in the U.S. government wanted such direct confrontation with the Soviets.

In addition, the United States had no significant business interests in Hungary. The United States also had to make decisions regarding the problems in the Suez Canal. The message was clear—it was not a good time for the United States to get involved. It offered only money to help the war-torn cities.

The free world had left the Hungarian people stranded. Hungary's hopes for choosing and keeping its own government were ruthlessly crushed. ■

Fidel Castro Leads Revolution in Cuba

On July 26, 1953, a young Cuban lawyer named Fidel Castro led a "suicide" charge in the province of Santiago de Cuba. He and a small group of followers attacked an army barracks. They were fighting to protest the policies of Cuba's dictator, Fulgencio Batista. They believed that Batista had taken power of Cuba illegally.

The attack did not succeed. Castro and some of his men were arrested and jailed. But the attack was not a complete failure for Castro. It helped make him a legend, and it started a political movement.

Since the beginning of the twentieth century, Cuba has been considered an important nation to the United States. Americans had once helped free Cuba from Spanish rule. The United States has had deep ties with the Cuban social and political community for years. The United States has helped Cuba financially. It has many business interests there.

By the early part of the 1950s, Cuba was considered a wealthy country. But that wealth was not spread over the whole population. The rich were very rich, but the poor were very poor. Sugar had once been a thriving business. As the decade progressed, however, sugar production declined drastically.

To make matters worse, the political system was in chaos. Since World War II, there had been many problems in Cuba with corrupt political leaders. Then Batista took power. Batista was a stern and cruel dictator. Many Cubans were unhappy with him. But opposition to his government was not organized. Fidel Castro changed all that. He was a strong and popular leader who pulled people to him. He inspired a few young men to follow him.

Castro's early defeats seemed to add romance and mystery to his cause . . .

After his July 26 attack and arrest, Castro spent two years in prison. But he didn't give up on his goal. He wanted to throw out Batista and his men for good. After he got out he formed another group of rebels and they began planning another assault on Batista's forces.

Early on, many of Castro's men were killed or jailed by Batista's government troops. At one point the rebels were beaten so badly that Castro was forced to retreat up into the hills with only a handful of men.

But these defeats only seemed to add romance and mystery to him, and to his cause. He became an even greater popular figure. He grew in stature in the eyes of young Cuban men and women looking to change Batista's policies.

Even in America, young people praised him as a fighter for freedom. Castro was, in fact, daring and brave. And he used his popular image and mystery to gain local support.

Batista Strikes Back Hard

In Cuba, more and more people became eager to help Castro's cause. In the cities, they supported the 26th of July Movement, as it was named after Castro's first attack.

The protests in the cities grew throughout the mid-1950s. So did Batista's opposition to them. He came down hard on his opponents. Many of them were jailed and tortured. This just made the protesters angrier and more determined.

Castro continued to fight his guerilla war against Batista's troops. Huge protests rocked cities throughout Cuba. To complicate matters for Batista, he was no longer getting the support he wanted from the United States. And when U.S. leaders found out that he was rigging elections, they knew they could not support him anymore.

Americans had their doubts about Castro. In the beginning, he was not openly communist. But then he started leaning more and more toward the Soviet Union. In fact, the

United States had hoped the Cubans would come up with someone else entirely. Both Batista *and* Castro were considered dangerous.

But it was far too late for compromises. Castro had gained overwhelming popular support. By mid-1958 Batista's government began to crumble. In January 1959, Batista fled the country. And by July of that same year, Castro openly celebrated the six-year anniversary of his popular movement.

As the decade ended, Fidel Castro was firmly in control of Cuba.

He has created some badly needed social reforms. But he has also angered the U.S. government by seizing American-owned sugar estates and cattle ranches and making them state-run businesses. As a result, relations between Cuba and the U.S. have declined sharply.

In turn, Castro has drifted closer and closer to the Soviet Union for aid and assistance. And the United States is now faced with the unhappy prospect of having a pro-Soviet government only 90 miles from its shores. ■

Fidel Castro waves triumphantly to cheering crowds as he enters Havana to take over the Cuban government. Castro seized control of the government from the dictator Batista.

An Old Soldier Fades Away

General Douglas MacArthur and President Harry Truman disagreed over the action the United States should take in the Korean War.

MacArthur had said, "There is no substitute for victory." He wanted to press on and attack Manchuria. If the United States went all out, he said, it could win the war. Then America could also establish itself as a major influence in the area for years to come.

But at what cost? Truman didn't want the U.S. to get bogged down in the Far East. He was getting a lot of pressure to end the war at the bargaining table—not on the battlefield.

So he said no to MacArthur's idea.

That was not unusual. Many arguments over strategy arise during a war. What was unusual was that

> MacArthur was a true leader . . . the trouble was, he did not *follow* well.

MacArthur tried to go around the president. He challenged Truman's U.S. foreign policy by taking his argument to the public.

The public loved Douglas MacArthur. They knew that this veteran of two world wars was tough and brave. They remembered his brilliant victory at Inchon. In the public's mind, politicians always talked and talked. But MacArthur was out there where the action was. He was a true leader.

The trouble was, he did not *follow* very well. So on April 11, 1951, Truman fired MacArthur and relieved him of his command. The president said that MacArthur was "unable to give his wholehearted support" to the policies of the U.S. government.

MacArthur was invited to address Congress when he returned from Korea in the spring of 1951.

MacArthur is given a hero's welcome in New York City.

MacArthur's admirers were shocked. In Japan, the Emperor showed up in person to say goodbye to the general. And a million Japanese lined the streets as the general was driven away.

The news reached home in a hurry. If MacArthur was a hero, Truman looked like a villain. Some people called for his impeachment! A dummy of Truman was burned in protest.

When MacArthur arrived home, he was given a hero's welcome. A parade and speeches were organized in his honor. Millions of people lined the parade route to show their support for him. Some people even urged him to challenge Truman in the next election. They did not seem to know or fully understand the seriousness of MacArthur's rebellion.

As commander-in-chief, the president is the head of all military forces. He has the last word. No matter how unpopular his order, all members of the military must obey that order. If they do not, chaos could result. In challenging Truman's policies, MacArthur undermined the president's authority.

Truman himself said that, ". . . military commanders must be governed by the policies and directives issued to them . . ."

Senate Asks Questions

Even General Dwight Eisenhower said, "When you put on a uniform there are certain (rules) you accept."

In the first few days after MacArthur arrived home, it looked as though Truman had made a big mistake. MacArthur was cheered practically every place he went. The general was even invited to give an address to Congress.

Then the Senate began to ask a lot of formal questions. The whole Korean War was open for debate. Was it being handled properly? Was Truman right? Was MacArthur right? Eventually the Senate sided with the president.

MacArthur did not enter politics as many had urged him to do. Perhaps he realized that the public forgets its heroes as quickly as it makes them. As he himself said in his farewell speech to Congress, "Old soldiers never die . . . they just fade away." And with those words, one of America's great military leaders retired from public life. ∎

The Rise and Fall of Joe McCarthy

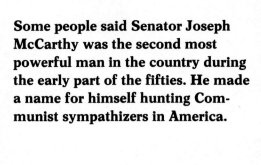

Some people said Senator Joseph McCarthy was the second most powerful man in the country during the early part of the fifties. He made a name for himself hunting Communist sympathizers in America.

By the end of World War II, the United States had become a rich and powerful country. Only one other nation could be considered its challenger—the Soviet Union. And Russia was a Communist state.

Communism had always frightened Americans. From its beginnings, the Communist party was thought of as dangerous to the American way of life. Communism meant revolution. It meant loss of freedom to speak out or practice religion. Even worse, Russia had the means and the power to spread communism to other countries. Americans wondered whether it could and would destroy the democratic way of life.

Senator Joseph McCarthy of Wisconsin was not the first politician to use communism as a means to a political end. Politicians from Woodrow Wilson to Vice-President Richard Nixon had also used it. They played upon Americans' fears of "Godless communism." But McCarthy was the first to use it with such sweeping personal success.

During the early 1950s only President Dwight Eisenhower was considered more powerful than the junior senator from Wisconsin. But Joseph McCarthy's political beginnings had not been grand. A poor farm boy, McCarthy had always wanted power. By determination and effort he worked and maneuvered his way from grocery-store manager to become a Wisconsin judge. Finally, he became a senator in 1947.

Until February 9, 1950, McCarthy's career in the senate had not been noteworthy. On that day, in Wheeling, West Virginia, McCarthy gave a speech to his fellow Republicans. He claimed that he had a "list of 205 names." The people listed were "known to the secretary of state as being members of the Communist party." Furthermore, he said that the people on that list were "working and shaping the policy of the State Department."

In truth, McCarthy had no such list of Communists. He was lying. But he found many true believers in the audience.

The facts were just as frightening as his fiction. The Communists had recently taken over Czechoslovakia and Hungary. They had blockaded West Berlin. They seemed to be stirring up trouble throughout the free world.

After World War II, some U.S. government employees had been shown to be Communist sympathizers. Others were convicted of various antigovernment crimes and sent to jail. If ever there was a time when Americans were ready to be frightened, this was it.

America's "Red Scare"

In later speeches, McCarthy toned down his accusations. The 205 Communists became simply "security risks." The number of offenders was then reduced to 81. Finally he referred to them only as "cases." But the seeds were already sown. America was in the midst of a "red scare." And Joseph McCarthy of Wisconsin was in control.

Some politicians tried to stop him. One man who tried was a senator up for re-election, Millard Tydings. He called McCarthy's list the hoax that it was. McCarthy had him ruined. He had a photo doctored so that it looked like Tydings was on friendly terms with a known Communist. He lost his re-election bid.

Only Eisenhower was considered more powerful than McCarthy.

Democrats feared McCarthy. Even the Republican Eisenhower was cautious of what he said about McCarthy in public. And most Republicans generally welcomed the man, if not his tactics. They had been out of power for twenty years. McCarthy was giving them some of that power back.

To get himself publicity, McCarthy went after anyone. He was not afraid of the rich and powerful in Washington. In fact, they were often his favorite targets.

". . . Those who have had all the benefits, the finest homes and educations, the finest jobs in government . . . the bright young men born with silver spoons in their mouths . . . they are the worst," he said.

McCarthy had two assistants to help him sniff out Communists. They were Roy Cohn and G. David Schine. In a series of Senate Committee hearings, this trio was responsible for hounding politicians and private citizens alike. The charges were always the same: having Communist "sympathies."

For more than three years McCarthy's attacks went unchecked. No one had the courage to stand up to him. Then in the fall of 1953, McCarthy went after the United States army. And for the first time in his career, the Wisconsin senator bit off a *lot* more than he could chew. ■

McCarthy is flanked by his two aides, Roy Cohn (right) and G. David Schine. In 1954 Cohn tried to pressure the military to give Schine a cushy post in the Army.

Roy Cohn (center) uses a blown-up photograph to prove a point during the Army-McCarthy hearings. Army counsel Joseph Welch is seated at the right.

McCarthy Exposed as "Power-Hungry" Bully

A young dentist named Irving Peress had been drafted by the army. Peress had refused to answer some questions on a standard loyalty form. So the army started its own investigation of him. The investigators found no skeletons in his closet. They just called him "left wing." When Peress asked for a discharge, the army gave it to him.

But for Joseph McCarthy, the matter was not closed. Peress had only been in the army a few short weeks. Still, he had been given the rank of an officer. McCarthy wanted

to know who had the nerve to promote such a man. Was it typical of the army to promote disloyal Americans? If so, perhaps the army itself was thick with "reds."

McCarthy called the commanding officer who had promoted Peress "ignorant" and a "disgrace." He told him he was not fit to be an officer. But McCarthy was not through. And neither was the army. They drafted one of McCarthy's aides—G. David Schine.

Roy Cohn, McCarthy's chief aide, was furious. He badgered the

32

army's top brass continually. He was trying to get his friend Schine an easy assignment in the service. Cohn even threatened to "wreck the army" if they did not do what he wanted. But the army exposed Cohn's actions. The *New York Times* of March 12, 1954, carried a story accusing Cohn of trying to pressure the army. "The army reported today that it had been subjected to direct threats by Senator Joseph McCarthy and his chief counsel, Roy Cohn."

McCarthy fought back. He said the army was purposely using Schine. He said they wanted to keep Schine from exposing all the corruption in the military. The Senate ordered hearings to sort out all the charges and countercharges.

A TV Audience of 20 Million

During the hearings, McCarthy and Cohn were on one side. On the other side was an attorney named Joseph Welch. He was representing the army. Welch was one of the "bright boys" McCarthy had earlier complained of. He came from a wealthy Bostonian family. Welch was as quiet and refined as McCarthy was loud and rough.

The hearings were very popular. They were televised daily to an audience of about 20 million Americans. The public found the Welch-McCarthy matchup great viewing.

In the hearings' early days McCarthy was in typical form. But as the days wore on, the tide turned against him.

Welch Strikes Back

One day, Joseph Welch was questioning Roy Cohn. He had Cohn on the ropes. His skillful questions were exposing Cohn and McCarthy as bullies. Cohn was stumbling and stuttering. He was struggling—as so many others had struggled in front of *him* over the past few years.

Sitting by Cohn's side, listening and growing impatient, was McCarthy. Suddenly he jumped in. He claimed that Welch's law firm employed a member of the Communist party named Fred Fisher.

McCarthy's statement was untrue. And what's more, it had nothing to do with the case before the Senate. McCarthy had just gotten angry and frustrated with Welch, so he picked on Fisher, a member of his law firm. Fisher was not even

present at the hearings. He could not defend himself against the charges.

Throughout the hearings until this point, Welch had been calm. But after listening to McCarthy's long-winded and mean-spirited attack, he changed his tone.

Welch said, "Until this moment, Senator, I never really gauged your cruelty or your recklessness. Fred Fisher is starting a brilliant career with us. Little did I dream you could be so reckless and so cruel to that fine lad. I fear he shall always bear a scar needlessly inflicted by you. . . . You have done enough! Have you no sense of decency at long last? Have you left no sense of decency?"

With that, Joseph Welch left the room in disgust. He also left millions of television viewers with a dramatic image: Joseph McCarthy as a blood-thirsty and power-hungry bully without principles. ⇨

A small group of loyal followers show their continued support for Senator McCarthy before heading for a rally in Washington D.C. in 1954. Later that year, the Senate stripped McCarthy of all his power.

Senate's action ends McCarthy's heyday.

The Red Scare was not over—but McCarthy's heyday was. Later that year the Senate voted 67 to 22 to censure McCarthy.

The condemnation did not remove him from office. He remained a senator for two more years. But the Senate's action stripped him of all his power, cutting off his "voice" to the public.

After losing his power, McCarthy began to keep to himself more and more. He became depressed and moody. His heavy drinking destroyed his liver. On May 2, 1957, he died.

It is true that Joseph McCarthy bullied and, at times, even lied his way to power. Some say he came closer than any man in American politics to wrecking the constitution. But the whole affair produced a triumph of decency in the person of Joseph Welch.

Upon hearing of McCarthy's death, Welch said, "I did not hate him. I am not good at hating any man." After all the damage McCarthy's tactics had done to the country, those were the kindest words he could have hoped for. ■

The Courage of One TV Journalist

Not everyone was taken in by Joseph McCarthy. By 1954, tens of thousands of Americans began to tire of his bullying and lies. But many more did not care to look behind the lies and get at the truth. They were swept up by the drama and they went along for the ride. They believed McCarthy must have had valid points to get so far.

At least one man had the power and the courage to say something for the silent masses of ordinary people. And he did.

His name was Edward R. Murrow. He was a newspaper writer, a war correspondent, and a radio and TV journalist. He had a television program called "See It Now."

On one show in March 1954, Murrow took on McCarthy. McCarthy was not in the studio with Murrow. But Murrow used actual film clips of the senator making speeches, and questioning his victims. And for every theatrical statement McCarthy made, Murrow countered with the cold facts.

It was the first time that anyone had publicly challenged McCarthy's half-truths on a point-by-point basis. McCarthy himself was not the cause of the fear and panic sweeping the country. According to Murrow he was just another sad symptom of it. On the same program Murrow went on to say, "We will not walk in fear of one another. We will not be driven by fear into an age of unreason. . . . We are not descended from fearful men. . . .

"The actions of (McCarthy) have caused alarm and dismay amongst our allies abroad and given comfort to our enemies. And whose fault is it? Not really his. He didn't create the situation of fear. He merely exploited it, and rather successfully."

Murrow had shown the American people another side of McCarthy. And what they saw scared them. The public's response was enormous. Thousands of telegrams poured in. Almost all of them were in agreement with Murrow. Most of them said things like, "Thank God somebody said something." ■

Journalist Edward R. Murrow exposed McCarthy's lies and tactics on his television program in March 1954.

The Rosenberg Controversy

The Spy Case of the Century

On June 19, 1953, Julius and Ethel Rosenberg died in the electric chair in New York's Sing Sing prison. They were executed for giving atomic secrets to the Soviet Union. At the time of their deaths, people all over the world protested. Many of them were sure the Rosenbergs were innocent. Others claimed that even if the couple were guilty, the death sentence was much too harsh. Even today, years later, the case still stirs controversy.

In 1943 Julius and Ethel Rosenberg were idealistic communists. Ethel's brother, David Greenglass, and his wife, Ruth, were also members of the Communist party. The four spoke passionately of their mutual Marxist cause. They were young and eager to change the world. The Rosenbergs often held Communist party meetings in their home.

At that time, Russia was an ally of the United States. Communist party members were asked to do their best to help end the war against Nazi Germany. During the war, a good number of U.S. citizens had ⇨

Julius and Ethel Rosenberg are taken into custody by U.S. officials in 1951. They were tried and convicted of passing U.S. atomic secrets to the Soviets.

communist sympathies. Communism had a different reputation than it had *after* the war.

When the war ended, Soviet Russia appeared to change. In the eyes of many Americans, Russia seemed to be playing the aggressor. To many, Russia seemed bent on world domination.

Public Fears Communists

More and more, America saw communists as a danger to national security. Many Americans believed that somehow communists seemed to have infiltrated every level of the U.S. government. In the election year of 1948, the Republicans had promised to rid the U.S. of these "fellow travelers." When Harry Truman was elected, he was pressured to expose Communist sympathizers in the government.

One of the first Communists to be caught was Klaus Fuchs. He had worked as a scientist on the "Manhattan Project" in the early 1940s. That was the top secret U.S. project that developed the atomic bomb.

In March 1950, Fuchs was arrested in Great Britain for violating British security laws. When he was caught, Fuchs also confessed that years before he had turned over secrets about the design of the A-bomb to the Russians.

In his confession, Fuchs said that he had given his secrets to a courier named Harry Gold. Somehow Fuchs and Gold, as well as others, had managed to slip through American security.

The U.S. government was worried. How far did this spy ring go? They wanted to identify the other spies. Perhaps they were still working for the Russians.

The FBI hunted down Harry Gold and caught him. When Gold confessed he began to name names. One of the names he mentioned was David Greenglass, Ethel Rosenberg's brother. Greenglass had also worked on the Manhattan Project.

When the FBI arrested Greenglass, he was so shaken up he also started naming names. He told the FBI about Julius and Ethel. He said they had asked him to pass secrets to the Russians.

According to Greenglass, Julius asked him to get secret information on the project. Julius said that he could then pass it on to the Russians. David agreed to do it.

The government said the Rosenbergs had stolen the "secret" of the atomic bomb.

Rosenberg told him a courier would visit the Greenglasses to pick up the secret information. David wondered how he would recognize this courier. Julius made up a signal that would assure David he was dealing with the right person.

Julius went into the kitchen and cut up a Jell-O box into two odd shapes. He kept one piece. The other piece would be given to the courier. The courier would in turn show this piece to the Greenglasses. That way, David and Ruth would know the courier was not setting a trap.

Later a courier did show up at the Greenglass home. He handed David the other piece of the Jell-O box. David knew this was the man Julius had told him about. David handed the courier secret materials from the Manhattan Project and some sketches. The courier in turn gave David $500.

David and Ruth Greenglass did not know at the time that the courier was Harry Gold. It was the same Harry Gold who had passed on the secrets from Klaus Fuchs.

The Case Hits a Dead End

In May 1950, the Rosenbergs were arrested. At first the FBI only arrested Julius. He seemed to be the important one. But Julius would not talk or name anyone else as fellow spies. In fact, all he would say was that his brother-in-law David was a liar. He denied all the charges against him.

The government wanted to know more. They had promised the American people that they would expose all the traitors.

Rosenbergs Won't Confess

The government's case was going well until they arrested Julius. His silence brought them to a dead end. They needed something to pressure him, to make him talk. So the FBI arrested his wife. They charged her with being his partner in crime. They thought he would crack if he knew she was in danger. Or maybe *she* would crack. In any case, one of them would surely start "singing." But the Rosenbergs did not sing. They maintained their innocence throughout the entire case.

During the trial, the affair became more and more overblown. What began as something moderate ended with much more serious accusations. By the end of the trial, the government's position was that the Rosenbergs had stolen the "secret" of the atomic bomb.

According to President Eisenhower, the damage that the Rosenbergs had done was "immeasurable." They could have "condemned to death millions of innocent people" by giving secrets to a power-hungry nation that seemed to want to rule the world. They had increased the chances of an "atomic war" with Russia.

On the attack, the government had created a real drama. But in defense of the Rosenbergs, an equally dramatic cry came from sympathizers. They said the Rosenbergs were innocent. They could never have pieced together such sophisticated atomic secrets. The government, they said, had set them up as fall guys.

But it became clear that Julius Rosenberg did organize a spy ring. And his wife Ethel at least *knew* about it. But no evidence ever sug-

gested she took an active part in any of Julius's activities. And beyond that, it was not clear at all how much damage Julius Rosenberg's *spy ring* had really done.

Though the spy ring was helpful to the Russians, it was not their only source of atomic secrets. But the government pressed hard anyway. The investigators wanted to expose as many spies as they could. They wanted the Rosenbergs to receive the death penalty to scare any other citizens who might be tempted to spy. This goal made them press too hard, some said.

But the government prosecutors were determined—the Rosenbergs were guilty, they claimed. A jury agreed. And the judge sentenced both Julius and his wife, Ethel, to death.

What angered the Rosenberg supporters most was the death sen-tence. They said even if the Rosenbergs were guilty, they were acting to help an *ally*—not an enemy. After all, they had passed the secrets during World War II when Russia was a friend of the United States. They noted that others convicted of the same type of crime had never received a death sentence.

From the time the trial ended, people all over the world pleaded for the couple's lives. Demonstrations were held in cities across America. Marches were even held outside the White House. But President Eisenhower refused to grant execu-tive clemency and spare their lives. The Rosenbergs went to their deaths calmly, protesting their innocence to the end.

Opinions about the case are still mixed. I. F. Stone, a journalist, wrote on July 2, 1956, "By American stand-

Many people who were uncertain of the Rosenbergs' guilt still felt their death sentence was too harsh. Here, protestors march outside the White House in January 1951, asking for presidential clemency.

ards, the Rosenberg case is unsatis-factory. . . . The Supreme Court never reviewed the case. The way the stay (of execution) was steamrolled was scandalous. The death sen-tence—even if they were guilty—was a crime."

Others disagree. They say the Rosenbergs had a fair trial, were guilty, and received a just sentence. One thing is certain. The controversy over the entire case of the "Atomic Spies" did not die with Julius and Ethel Rosenberg. ■

President Eisenhower and Vice-President Nixon join their wives to greet Republican delegates at the party's national convention.

America Likes Ike

Eight Years of Peace and Prosperity

The Republicans were "hungry." They had been kept out of the White House since 1932. Democrat Franklin Delano Roosevelt had been elected president four times, and had served 12 years. When he died at the beginning of his fourth term, Vice-President Harry Truman became president. He finished out FDR's term, and then won his own term in 1948.

Truman's last few years in office had been tough. The Korean War had gone on too long. Attempts at peace failed. Thousands of American GIs had been killed. Truman fired MacArthur, a popular war hero, but he seemed unable to stop the war with his own plan.

To make matters worse, communism was on everyone's lips. Congress became obsessed with attempts to expose spies and traitors at all levels of government. After 20 years in office, the Democrats appeared to have outstayed their welcome.

In 1952 the Republicans chose Dwight David Eisenhower to lead them back to the White House. Eisenhower had been supreme allied commander in Europe. He was a popular figure, a war hero. Yet his image was not warlike. He was known as a top-notch organizer. He had used brains more than brawn during World War II. He was a man of peace.

No one associated him with a political party. Eisenhower himself didn't even have a set of political objectives. But Americans sensed that "Ike," as he was called, was a nice guy. In fact, his campaign slogan was "I like Ike." He promised to build a "better future for America."

People wanted to see themselves in Eisenhower—simple, good,

Eisenhower remained in office for the next eight years. He won re-election easily in 1956, defeating Stevenson for a second time. During his two terms, the United States experienced great economic recovery and growth.

One of the first things Eisenhower did was to end the war in Korea. That cemented his popularity. Ending the war had been one of his most important campaign promises. When he came through, the American people knew he could be trusted.

Eisenhower was a man who always looked in control. He accomplished this by delegating and being open to compromise. Eisenhower saw himself as above party squabbles. He saw himself as running the country the way he ran the army, with a strong even hand.

He was so popular that at one time he claimed the Republicans could have control in the United States "forever." In July 1955 the *New*

York Times reported Eisenhower as saying, "a properly unified party could retain control of the national Administration forever."

A "Modern" President

"Modern Republicanism," Eisenhower said, "looks to the future." This means it will constantly gain new recruits. It will increase in power and influence for years to come."

"Modern" was the key word. Americans responded well to all things "modern." Ike was a "modern" president for "modern" times.

Eisenhower did have some critics. Some saw him as lazy. He seemed forever to be playing golf. ⇨

There were more than three million golfers in the United States during the decade. The most famous lived in the White House for eight years— Dwight D. Eisenhower.

In 1952 America wanted simple answers, simple solutions.

hard working, and brave. What they did not want to see was another politician cut from the same cloth as all the rest. They were tired of the same old slogans and causes. The old guard had gotten them into two wars and some major economic troubles. In 1952 Americans wanted simple answers, simple solutions.

The Democrats' choice was Adlai Stevenson, the governor of Illinois. Stevenson was more of the typical politician. He was a brilliant man, an intellectual. Some people called him an "egghead." His speeches were intelligent, wise, and witty. But his answers to problems seemed too complex. As a result, Eisenhower was elected by a landslide.

Ike's easygoing style suited most Americans.

But so was a large part of the population. Most Americans thought his golf playing was just fine.

Americans had time on their hands again. Most adults couldn't remember what that felt like. They had lived through the depression. They had fought in one, or even two, wars. But now things were changing. Life felt good again. And Ike was the easygoing type of leader that suited their life style. Even Eisenhower's heart attack in 1955 didn't weaken his image as a strong leader.

Eisenhower had helped advance the cause of Negro rights. He had at least begun to meet the Soviet challenge in space and technological research. He had increased federal spending for education. And the gross national product had broken all existing records. By the end of the decade, nearly 50% of all families were earning more than $5,000 a year.

There was no doubt about it. America liked Ike. ∎

A Vice President and His Dog

Richard M. Nixon was Eisenhower's vice president from 1952 to 1960. During both of Eisenhower's campaigns for the presidency, Republicans considered dumping Nixon from the ticket.

Nixon's major problems arose during the first run for control of the White House. He was accused of accepting illegal campaign contributions. There was no doubt that Nixon *did* take money. With the help of an old friend, he had organized a group of backers who put money into a "permanent campaign fund."

Nixon's salary was "pitifully inadequate," the backers said. He needed help and they gave it to him. Nixon insisted that the fund was not a secret. He said it was legal, but many people challenged that.

Republicans and Democrats alike began to doubt his word. Everywhere he went, Nixon found himself defending the fund. Eisenhower's bid for the presidency was in danger of getting bogged down in Nixon's problems. Some Republicans wanted Nixon to step down. But Nixon chose to fight it out—on television.

In a TV speech, on September 23, 1952, he went before the American people to deny that he had done anything wrong. He said he did not try to keep the fund a secret, and none of the money went for his personal use. He denied granting favors to the people who gave him the money.

He added that he had not "feathered his nest." To prove it, he listed everything he owed.

He said, "(My wife) and I know that every dime we've got is honestly ours . . . . She doesn't have a mink coat. But she does have a respectable Republican cloth coat."

He admitted to taking one gift—a dog named Checkers. "Our kids love the dog," he told the TV audience. "And I just want to say this right now, that regardless of what they say about it, we are going to keep (Checkers)."

Nixon said it really was not up to him to stay in, or step down from the campaign. That decision belonged to the Republican National Committee. He urged the people of America to send telegrams and letters to the committee supporting him.

Many people remained unconvinced. They said Nixon had not been completely truthful even in his TV address. But these people were not in the majority.

In September 1952, Richard Nixon addressed the nation on television to answer charges about his "expense fund." The address, later to become known as the "Checkers speech," saved Nixon's political career.

His speech worked. The remark about the dog, Checkers, seemed to show that Nixon was just another working Joe—a husband, a father, a sentimental guy. Thousands of wires and letters came in. Thousands of telephone calls were made. Almost all of them were in support of Nixon. They urged the Republican National Committee to keep him on the ticket. Eisenhower was convinced, too. When he met Nixon after the TV speech he threw his arm around him and said, "You're my boy." And the rest, as they say, is history. ∎

Devastating Diane

Since Helen of Troy, few women's names have put more fear in the hearts of men. She hit the country in 1955, literally laying waste to a good part of the East Coast. She twisted up steel railroad tracks as if they were pipe cleaners. She picked up cars and threw them down miles away. She killed more than 400 people and left more than 70 "missing" before she was through. She caused the worst flooding in U.S. history.

She was Hurricane Diane.

The relationship between Diane and America didn't last long, but it was marked by great tragedy. It was August 18 when she first kicked up her heels. The winds were terrible. But the rains that followed were even worse. They flooded parts of Pennsylvania, New York, New Jersey, and Massachusetts. And Connecticut was declared a disaster area.

The Delaware River rose to a record height. Muddy waters carried away whole bridges and washed away highways. Dams were smashed. Factories and homes were destroyed. An entire section of a building was ripped from its foundation and carried away.

In Connecticut the flooding was the worst ever. The Naugatuck River, racing at 50 mph, rose and destroyed dams. Total damage from Diane's "visit" in Connecticut alone, was more than one billion dollars. More than 30,000 people were left without jobs or homes.

All in all, as far as the East Coast was concerned, Diane was not a very nice lady. ∎

Hurricane Diane swept up the east coast in the summer of 1955. More than 400 people lost their lives, and property worth millions of dollars was destroyed.

Local laws in the south forced Negroes to use separate facilities from whites.

Negroes Fight for Civil Rights

The fifties were a time of comfortable prosperity. At last the economy was back on track! After the hardships caused by both World War II and Korea, the American people were enjoying a time of growth. Workers were saving time on the job because of new technology. Housewives were saving time because of new appliances. In general, life was getting easier.

For one section of the American population, however, life was not so easy or pleasant. Negro Americans were still experiencing many hardships. Most good jobs were not open to them, and they still earned less money than whites. Often they lived in dangerous and dirty parts of the cities. And most frustrating of all, they were not allowed the same basic rights as white people.

The United States Constitution had spelled out those rights clearly. But private businesses, individuals, and state and local governments did not always go along with the Constitution. As a result, Negroes were treated as second-class citizens.

Generally speaking, Negroes didn't get fair treatment anywhere in America. But in the South, the problems between black and white people were terrible. There were separate facilities for blacks and whites everywhere in the South. There were schools for whites and schools for blacks, bathrooms for whites and bathrooms for blacks. Even water fountains were labeled for whites and blacks. This had been the way of life for years. Most southerners accepted it. But Negroes resented being treated this way.

One woman who resented it was Rosa Parks. She was a seamstress who worked in Montgomery, Alabama. On December 1, 1955, she had worked especially hard all day. She was tired. All she wanted was to get on the bus, find a seat, and rest. Luckily for her, she found a seat.

But in that part of Alabama, Negro riders were required by law to give up their seats if whites wanted to sit down. When a white man asked Rosa Parks to give up her seat, she refused. Somehow, at that moment, she had had enough. But by refusing to give up her seat, she broke the law. So she was arrested.

Boycott the Buses!

The Negro community was furious. The years of resentment that had built up exploded like a volcano. If an American citizen could get arrested for sitting down, it was time to make some changes.

Mrs. Parks went to trial. She was convicted and fined. Tensions mounted. Mrs. Parks appealed her case. A group of Negro women went to their local preachers with an idea. If the bus companies treated Negroes badly, then perhaps Negroes should not ride the buses at all. So they decided to boycott the buses.

The preachers thought the boycott was a good idea. The organizers

of the action made it clear that Negroes would continue to stay off the buses until things changed. They wanted bus drivers to be courteous to Negroes. They wanted passengers to be seated first come, first serve. And they wanted Negroes to be given jobs as bus drivers along routes through Negro neighborhoods.

The Supreme Court said that Rosa Parks had a right to sit down and keep her seat.

The Montgomery city officials said no to their demands. So the boycott went on. City leaders didn't think the boycott was going to be successful. But a large percentage (about 75%) of bus riders were Negro. Soon the bus lines were losing thousands of dollars.

The boycott was hard on the riders, too. In order to help Negroes get to jobs and markets, a special car pool was organized. One of the

organizers was Dr. Martin Luther King, Jr. He and his fellow preachers did everything they could to keep the people strong and their spirits high.

It turned into a lengthy boycott. Hundreds of days passed. The bus companies held on, and Negroes had a hard time getting around. When Rosa Parks lost her first appeal, she took her case to the United States Supreme Court.

Meanwhile, the city officials struck back. They said that King's car pool was an illegal transport service. He and his fellow preachers were arrested and jailed.

In late 1956, things looked bad. The boycott had already lasted more than 380 days. People had grown tired and scared. They wondered if things would ever change. Then the U.S. Supreme Court made a historic ruling. It said that Alabama's state and local laws requiring segregation on buses were unconstitutional. It said Rosa Parks had a right to sit down and keep her seat.

The boycott had worked. The next day, Negroes rode the buses. And although there had been some outbreaks of violence earlier, everything was now peaceful. Rosa Parks had waged a small fight for a simple human dignity. And she had won a major battle for civil rights. ■

Some big events start out small. Rosa Parks refused to give up her seat to a white man in Montgomery, Alabama, and was arrested and convicted. But a year later, in December of 1956, her protests helped change the law.

A Crisis in the Schools

Integration Stirs Trouble

On September 15, 1957, U.S. National Guardsmen were ordered to safely escort nine Negro students into an all-white Arkansas high school.

The bus boycott was just one victory for civil rights. The Supreme Court had made it clear that Negroes and whites had equal rights. But the fact was that Negroes were still separated from the white population in many areas. This problem was very obvious in school systems throughout the country. Both in the North and the South, many schools were still segregated.

This was true despite the fact that in 1954 the U.S. Supreme Court had ruled that segregated schools were unconstitutional. But many state and local officials in the North and South had continued to ignore the Court's ruling.

Of course, it wasn't just officials who didn't want schools integrated. Many white students flatly rejected the idea of sharing classes with Negro students.

Miss Autherine J. Lucy struggled for three years to get into the University of Alabama. Finally she was accepted. But she was suspended when a group of rowdy white stu-

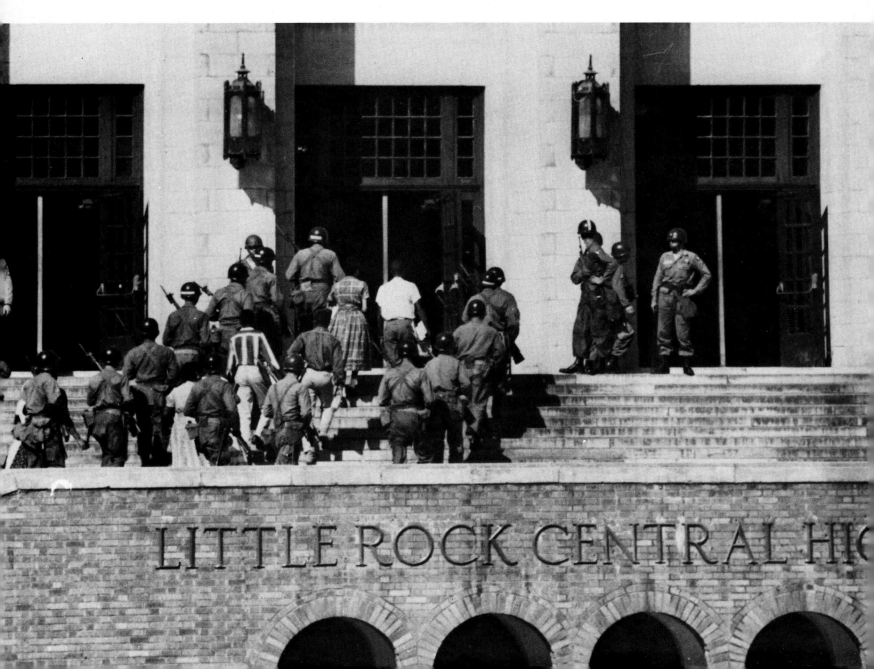

dents protested her presence. Many people claimed that she had been taken from the school for her own safety. They said she might have been killed by angry white mobs.

Later she was readmitted. But the incident was used by both whites and blacks to prove a point. Negroes said the case was proof that Negroes were denied certain basic rights under the law. And whites claimed that the presence of Negroes in the schools would only disrupt order and cause violence.

Soldiers clutched their rifles. Students clutched their schoolbooks. Together they entered the school.

The federal government tried to enforce integration, but it wasn't easy. In Little Rock, Arkansas, the problem came to a dramatic climax. September 4, 1957, was to be the first day of integration for Central High School. Nine Negro students were to attend an all-white high school. But Arkansas governor Orval Faubus, did not agree with the idea of integration. He sent the National Guard to Central High, saying they were there "to preserve order." Instead the National Guard blocked the nine Negro students from going inside.

Eisenhower Sends in Troops

Later in the month, the National Guard was removed. The nine Negro students finally got inside the school.

But hundreds of angry white students threatened to lynch them if they didn't leave. For their own safety, they left the school.

Finally on September 25, 1957, President Eisenhower had to send thousands of soldiers to Little Rock. These troops were ordered to get the nine students safely inside the school. Soldiers clutched their rifles. Students clutched their schoolbooks. Together they entered the school.

It was a tense moment. But a message had been delivered. The U.S. government would do whatever was necessary, including the use of force, to insure the constitutional rights of minorities.

Not everyone was happy with the federal government's position. Governor Faubus had defied the president all along. He had been *forced* to accept integration whether he agreed with it or not.

Faubus told his people that he would continue to fight the federal government. He said, "General Lee

Miss Authurine Lucy won a three-year battle to attend the previously all-white University of Alabama.

was offered command of the (Union) Army. But he remained loyal to the people of his state. The Democratic party of the North wants me to go along with them on the integration issue. I will remain with the people of Arkansas."

Many people all over the country agreed with Faubus. Negroes and their supporters had won another battle. But the fight for civil rights would continue. The day of Faubus's speech, the *New York Times* reported, "It was a quiet day in Little Rock. The nine Negro boys and girls attended school without incident. But no early solution to the crisis seemed likely." ∎

The Man in the Glass Booth

Week after week, TV viewers looked forward to seeing him sweating away in his soundproof booth. He was young, clean-cut, and very intelligent. His name was Charles Van Doren. People thought he was a boon to American education and a guiding light to teachers. In every way he seemed to be a model young person—the kind of man every mother hoped her daughter would marry. The trouble was he was also a cheat.

Quiz shows were very big in the early days of television. Most of them were honest. But some of them were rigged. One of the dishonest shows was called "Twenty One."

Two contestants fought each other in a battle of wits. They were each asked a question. Each question was worth money and points. Easy questions were worth a few points and a little money. Hard questions gained the contestant lots of points and a great deal of money. If contestants answered correctly, they got the money and points and could continue. If they answered wrong, they were out of the competition.

The audience did not know it at the time, but some contestants were given answers to the questions ahead of time. Charles Van Doren was one of those chosen few.

The producers of the show asked Van Doren to help them with the fraud. Their idea was simple. If the audience liked a contestant and could identify with him, they'd watch the show. And the more people who watched, the more money the show could charge for commercials.

The producers figured it was good business to keep likable contestants on for a long time. Since contestants had to keep answering questions to stay on, the producers decided to tell them the answers ahead of time.

Van Doren was a likable guy. He was an English teacher who taught at a very good university. He managed to attract a big following and he also won big money— $129,000.

Herb Stempel was another fake winner. Only Herb blew the whistle on the producers of "Twenty One." He went to the district attorney. The D.A. opened an investigation of "Twenty One" and other quiz shows.

The investigation turned up more cases of quiz show fraud. Many producers were disgraced. Van Doren lost his job. And TV viewers changed channels. ∎

Charles Van Doren admitted that he had been given answers ahead of time by the producers of "Twenty One."

Edmund Hillary
On Top of the World

In June 1953 Elizabeth was about to be crowned queen of England. As she waited, she heard the news. Edmund Hillary, a British subject, had succeeded in reaching the peak of Mount Everest—the world's tallest mountain. A runner from Hillary's expedition raced the news from the expedition's base camp to a nearby village. The message was a kind of coronation gift for Elizabeth II.

Mount Everest is situated on the borders of Nepal and Tibet. It was named after the British surveyor general of India, Sir George Everest.

Two Failed Attempts

Edmund Hillary lives in New Zealand. He keeps bees and climbs mountains. He and his Sherpa guide, Tenzing Norgay, were the first men ever to reach Everest's peak. Norgay was a veteran climber. He had been on other expeditions before. But nothing could compare with climbing Everest.

It was the third try for Hillary and his guide. Twice before they had tried to scale the mountain and had failed. The month of May means spring in many parts of the world. But that is not the case at 29,000 feet. Bitter cold and deadly winds are a constant reality in the Himalayas. Hillary's team was the eleventh to try to conquer the world's tallest mountain. In past expeditions many climbers had died in the attempt.

Hillary's bold expedition had been a struggle from the start. The expedition team numbered more than 300 men who carried the 10,000 pounds of baggage to the base camp and beyond.

Hillary also took with him 20 Sherpa guides, including Norgay. The trek began in March and took 80 days to complete. Hillary claimed the mountain in honor of the new queen. He planted the British Union Jack and the flag of Nepal on the peak. ∎

Edmund Hillary, right, and his sherpa guide, Tenzing Norgay, became the first men ever to set foot atop Mt. Everest, the highest mountain in the world.

47

Antiwar Message Reaches Millions

Schweitzer Speaks Out

Albert Schweitzer holds the child of an African villager. In 1958 the noted humanitarian warned the world of atomic disaster.

Albert Schweitzer has many talents to share with the world. He is a musician, a philosopher, a theologian, a physician, and a missionary. He is an authority on Bach. He has written many books and essays.

But of all the things Albert Schweitzer has given us, perhaps the greatest is hope. In 1952 he won the Nobel Peace Prize for a lifetime of humanitarian work.

Schweitzer used the money that came with the prize to build a hospital for lepers in French Equatorial Africa. As a doctor, he treats the body. But he is also a healer of the human spirit. His goal is to help people mend the damage caused by fear and hatred.

Perhaps Schweitzer's most important contribution came in a warning. The following is part of a radio address he issued to the world in April 1958.

"Since March 1954, hydrogen bombs have been tested by the United States. After the explosion of a hydrogen bomb, something remains in the air—a number of (harmful) radioactive particles. . . .

"We are being told about (safe levels) of this radiation. What does (safe) mean? And who has the right to permit people to be exposed to these dangers?

"Today we are faced with the possibility of an outbreak of atomic war between Soviet Russia and the United States. It can only be (stopped) if the two powers decide to (give up) atomic arms. . . .

"In an atomic war, both sides would suffer the same fate. . . . The radioactive clouds that would result from a war between the East and West would (harm) humanity everywhere.

"In President Eisenhower's speech of November 7, 1957, we find the following: 'What the world needs more than a gigantic leap into space is a gigantic leap into peace.'

"The gigantic leap consists in finding the courage to hope. To hope that a spirit of good sense will arise in all peoples. (We need) a spirit strong enough to overcome the insanity and the inhumanity."

Schweitzer has devoted his entire life to the brotherhood of man. His 1952 Nobel Prize was international recognition of his lifelong efforts to help the world's less fortunate people. He continues to have a strong, moral influence over people throughout the world. ■

Sputnik and the Space Grapefruit

On October 4, 1957, Sputnik I could be seen clearly in the night sky. At about 23 inches wide and 184 pounds, it glided overhead like a shooting star. It should have been a beautiful sight. And indeed, to the Soviet Union, which launched the unmanned satellite, it was.

But as Sputnik I exploded 560 miles into space, American dreams exploded with it. The United States had long prided itself on being first in technology. Now, in the new frontier of space, America was second best.

It was only after Josef Stalin died that Americans had their first real glimpse of Russia. What they saw were little men in old-fashioned suits. How could they do much of anything? Americans laughed at their outdated cars and equipment. But the laughing stopped when Sputnik conquered the sky.

Long before Sputnik I, both Russians and Americans had been busy building space-type rockets. In the Soviet Union, K. E. Tsiolkovsky pioneered multistage rocket design. In America, Robert Goddard worked on his rockets alone. His experiments didn't arouse much interest. It wasn't until 1955 that the United States got involved in intensive space research.

No sooner had the United States recovered from the blow of Sputnik I, than another Sputnik was launched. In November 1957 Sputnik II shot into orbit. This time it carried a dog and stayed in orbit for almost half a year.

America didn't have a successful space launch until February 1958. Explorer 1 was much smaller than Sputnik, but it reached more than twice the altitude—1,600 miles up.

Later, America's tiny Vanguard 1 was launched. Russia's premier Khrushchev referred to it as a little "grapefruit." Vanguard made a successful orbit. And it also provided important details about the earth and its atmosphere. It was one of the most significant launches in space history.

Many scientists had once put space travel in the realm of science fiction. Now they knew it was no longer fiction. It was fact. And the race for space was on. ∎

The Russian earth satellite Sputnik I, shown mounted on a stand, orbited the earth in October 1957.

The Shot Heard 'Round the World: Delirious New York Giant players mob hero Bobby Thomson as he crosses home plate after hitting a pennant-winning three-run homer in the 1951 playoffs against the Brooklyn Dodgers.

Next Year Finally Arrived For Brooklyn's 'Bums'

"Wait till *next* year." That was the battle cry—year after year—for Brooklyn Dodgers fans. But it was cold comfort to those millions of Dodgers supporters who backed the team each year. For in the end, the Dodgers couldn't win the big games when it counted.

The frustrating thing was that for years the team had fine talent. No one could deny that. They had come a long way since their early years. In those days the team was so bad that they rightfully earned the nickname used even today—Bums. Since the early 1940s, the Dodgers had put a pretty good team on the field each season. Brooklyn won the National League Pennant in 1941, 1947, and 1949. But each time they lost the World Series to their rivals, the New York Yankees.

Seeing them lose year after year brought a community of fans together. And seeing the Yankees win year after year created a common enemy. For Brooklyn fans it wasn't just a game—it was life.

The fifties were the worst of

times and the best of times for Dodgers fans. In 1950 the World Series went to the Yankees. They swept the National League's Philadelphia Phillies in four games.

The 1951 series saw the Yankees win again, this time defeating the New York Giants in six games. Although the Giants were the Dodgers fierce league rival, some Brooklyn fans were cheering for them. They just wanted anyone to beat the Yankees.

Most Dodgers fans, however, were probably quite happy to see the Giants lose. For it was the Giants who knocked the Dodgers right out of the National League pennant that year.

The two teams had finished the '51 season in a tie. Each team had won two games of the playoffs to decide the pennant. The Dodgers led the final game 4–2 in the ninth inning. Then the Giants' Bobby Thomson hit a three-run home run over the left field fence at the Polo Grounds. His "shot heard round the world" crushed the Dodgers and sent all of Brooklyn into mourning. Of course, the Giants felt pretty good about it.

In 1952 the Yankees were once again American League champions. But this time, the Dodgers won the National League pennant. They squared off with the Yankees in the World Series and lost again—this time in seven games.

The next year would prove to be more of the same. Another victory for the Yankees—another defeat for the National League champs, the Dodgers. It was the seventh World Series defeat in Dodgers' history—the last five to the Yankees.

No Dodger or Yankee fan can remember just what happened in 1954. Word has it that Willie Mays and the Giants flattened Cleveland, winning the Series in four straight.

Then in 1955 a wonderful thing happened. In 1955 the *world changed*. Yes, the Yankees took the American League pennant. Nothing unusual there. And yes, the Dodgers won the National League flag. That could have been expected as well. What happened next, well, *that* was something to behold. The Bums were about to become kings.

It was a hard battle. It took hitting from Dodger starts like Duke Snider, Gil Hodges, Carl Furillo and Roy Campanella. And pitchers like Johnny Podres, who shut out the Yankees in the final game.

After the final out, the crowd went crazy. The Bums had *finally* beaten the Yankees. In a matter of seconds, the field was overrun with fans. It was a moment they had never before witnessed. The Dodgers were World Champs!

All of Brooklyn celebrated the Dodgers' victory. In fact, the New York borough of three million people went wild with joy. People said they hadn't seen such celebrating since the end of World War II.

The next year the two teams were at it again. But the 1956 Series would be remembered for the accomplishment of one man—Yankee pitcher Don Larsen. In game five, Larsen pitched a *perfect* game. No Dodger player reached first base—not on a hit, a walk, or an error. It was the first time in Series history that a pitcher had been "perfect."

The Dodgers fought back. They took it to the wire. They finally lost

Dodger players and fans celebrate the final out of the 1955 World Series. After decades of futility, the "Bums" were finally World Champs, defeating their hated rivals, the Yankees, in seven games.

the championship in seven games to the Yankees. Brooklyn fans didn't know it at the time, but that was their last appearance in the Series.

After the 1957 season, the Dodgers left Brooklyn and moved to California. They sought the sunny weather (and "better" playing condi-

tions) of Los Angeles. The Giants went with them and settled up north, in San Francisco. Giants and Dodgers fans were heartbroken. Baseball in New York would never again be the same. And the cries of "Wait till next year" and "dem Bums," became only fading echos in a dark, empty ballpark. ∎

The first of many perfect pitches: Don Larsen made World Series history in 1956 by becoming the first hurler ever to pitch a perfect game in the Series.

Two Stars Shine at the 1952 Olympics

The Olympics had been put on hold during the war years. Then in 1948, the games were resumed, this time in London. But Germany and Japan were not present. And the Soviet Union was not yet a part of the International Olympic Committee.

In 1952 things got back to normal. The summer games were held in Helsinki, Finland, and the winter games in Oslo, Norway. Germany, Japan, and Russia all competed. The games took on some of their old feeling again.

At the summer games, the Helsinki crowd was happy and enthusiastic. Opening day ceremonies drew a crowd of 70,500. A total of 69 nations were present and 6,000 men and 800 women athletes competed in 17 different sports. In 19 of 24 events,

Olympic records were broken. The U.S. team did well, its men winning 14 gold medals in their track and field events.

But some of the most remarkable victories belonged to a Czechoslovakian runner. His name was Emil Zatopek. Without a doubt, he was the star of the games.

Zatopek's running style was hardly free and easy. He was actually hard to watch. His face was always edged with pain. But even though he *looked* like he was struggling, his racing times—and the race results— said otherwise.

Zatopek competed in three track events in Helsinki: the 5,000 meter, the 10,000 meter, and the marathon. The pressure was on in the 10,000 meter race. He had won the event

four years earlier. Could he do it again? He did—and broke his own 1948 Olympic record by 42 seconds!

Zatopek faced his toughest field in the 5,000 meter event. In the 1948 Olympics he had finished second in the event. But this time he edged out Alain Mimoun of France to win and set another record. That same day, Zatopek's wife, Dana, took a gold medal in the javelin.

The Olympic marathon was Emil Zatopek's first ever. But he easily won that event too, by two-and-a-half minutes. Zatopek won gold medals in all three long-distance track events—and set world record times in each race. It was one of the greatest feats in Olympic history.

The star of the 1952 winter games in Oslo was skier Andrea Mead Lawrence of the United States. Though a fall caused her to lose the downhill to Austria's Trude Jochum-Beiser, Lawrence still came up a winner in two other major events. She took a gold medal in both the slalom and the giant slalom. Lawrence thus became the first woman ever to win two winter Olympic gold medals. ∎

In the 1952 Winter Olympics, American skier Andrea Mead Lawrence took a gold medal in both the slalom and giant slalom.

The 1952 Summer Olympics belonged to Emil Zatopek. The Czechoslovakian won gold medals in three different track events. He also set new world records in each race.

Sweet and Deadly in the Ring

His nickname is Sugar Ray—the "sweetest fighter . . . sweet as sugar," as a sportswriter described him years ago. But for nearly 15 years, Sugar Ray Robinson has not only been sweet. He's been tough, smooth, fast—and a champion boxer. After being undefeated in 89 amateur bouts, Robinson won the professional welterweight title in 1946.

Sugar Ray held that crown for five years. Then in 1951 he fought the reigning middleweight champ, Jake LaMotta. They had fought once before, and LaMotta had broken Robinson's string of 40 straight professional victories.

This time the story was different. In a memorable and brutal battle on February 14, 1951, Robinson knocked out LaMotta in the thirteenth round to win the middleweight crown. Robinson then gave up his welterweight title and continued to fight as a middleweight for the rest of the decade.

Throughout the 1950s, Sugar Ray lost his title several times. But each time he regained the championship in a rematch with the fighter who had taken it from him. In all, he won the middleweight title on five separate occasions.

Throughout his career, Robinson has been a popular figure both inside and outside the ring. His style of boxing (smooth, quick, and yet a punishing hitter) has gained him acclaim from boxing experts everywhere. And his colorful, flamboyant personality has gained him fame even outside the prizefighting world.

Sugar Ray Robinson has been a champion at some professional boxing level for nearly 15 years. He may go down as the greatest all-around fighter in history. ∎

The hammering right hand of Sugar Ray Robinson forces Jake LaMotta to duck in the third round of their championship fight, in 1951.

Queen of the Court

She started out on the streets of Harlem and wound up shaking hands with the queen of England. Her name is Althea Gibson. And in the late 1950s she dominated the world of women's tennis.

Althea Gibson was born in South Carolina, but she grew up in New York City. She learned to play tennis using a wooden paddle on the sidewalks of Harlem. "I had to be tough," she said. "I could fight. My daddy taught me all the moves."

Althea took her toughness with her onto the tennis court. For ten

Althea Gibson returns a serve at the 1957 Wimbledon tournament.

straight years (1947-1956), she was the singles champion in the American Tennis Association competition for Negro players.

In 1956 Althea gained sudden fame by winning her first major tournament. That year she captured the French singles and doubles titles.

In 1957 and 1958 Althea became famous throughout the sports world. In both years she won the U.S. Open titles and the British titles at Wimbledon. She became the first Negro ever to win a Wimbledon title.

In recognition of her accomplishments, Althea was named by the Associated Press as the outstanding woman athlete of the year for both 1957 and 1958. ∎

Movie star James Dean was a symbol of the 1950s teenage rebel.

The Birth and Death of the Cool

One plays a horn. The other starred in motion pictures. They both won fame and popularity all over the world. And they both have come to symbolize the "cool" generation of the fifties. Their names are Miles Davis and James Dean.

James Byron Dean was born in Indiana in 1931. He moved with his family to Los Angeles at a young age. When his mother died, he moved back to the Midwest where he was raised by relatives.

After high school he returned to L.A. to study with a small theater group. He did a few TV commercials and appeared in bit parts in movies. But his serious acting began when he moved to New York City. There he worked as a busboy and took acting classes at night.

Finally, in 1954, he got his big break. When he appeared in a play called "The Immoralist," a Hollywood director saw him, liked him, and signed him to a movie contract.

In a little more than a year, Dean appeared in three very popular films. He came to be a symbol of the angry young man—the rebel. The restless teens of the fifties could identify with him. James Dean talked the way they talked. He behaved the way they wanted to behave. The characters he played were sensitive, moody perhaps, and a little wild. And they were always misunderstood by the adult world.

Dean will probably be remembered best as the *Rebel Without A Cause*. His stardom was certain after *East of Eden*. Dean's last picture, *Giant* was released in 1956. By that time the legend—and tragedy—of James Dean had become a permanent part of popular culture.

On September 30, 1955, Dean was driving his $7,000 Porsche Speedster to Salinas, California, to compete in a race. But he never made it. On his way he crashed into another car and was killed. His death shocked Hollywood and devastated his millions of fans everywhere.

Though his stardom was very brief, the years that have passed since Dean's death have not erased his memory. Each year, his popularity grows. In many ways he represented the ideal '50s young rebel whose creed was once expressed by another movie teenager: "Live fast, die young, and have a good-looking corpse."

The other symbol of fifties cool probably cannot be called a rebel. But like the late James Dean, Miles Davis is unique—unlike the hundreds of jazz trumpeters who have come before him.

Davis's 1950 album, "Birth of the Cool" says it all. It almost single-handedly gave birth to "cool" jazz. Since then, Davis has nurtured the music and sent it on its way into the clubs and recording studios of America.

Davis plays like a silk shirt feels.

Miles Dewey Davis was born in 1926 and raised in East St. Louis. One of his father's dental patients became Davis's first music teacher. Davis studied the basics of classical music, but the teacher also introduced him to the music of the best jazz trumpeters.

In the 1940s he continued his classical training at the Julliard School of Music in New York. But by then he had a strong desire to play jazz. So he began frequenting all the jazz clubs in New York. Soon, he was sitting in with many of the best groups around, including the one led by the legendary Charlie Parker.

In the late 1940s, Davis formed his own nine-piece group and began innovating. He put together combinations of instruments not usually linked with jazz. French horn and alto sax were played beside trumpet and piano.

Over the years Davis has become known for his crisp, clear tone of playing. He has a style that sounds like a silk shirt feels. But he is also known as a keen student and a gen-erous teacher. He has helped and encouraged other great jazz artists and has showcased dozens more.

In the early '50s drugs and alcohol threatened to ruin his young career. But he kicked his habits and went on to become a hit again when he played at the 1955 Newport Jazz festival. After that he was offered a recording contract.

In the late '50s, Davis formed a new jazz quintet that featured the young, talented, tenor saxophonist, John Coltrane. The group has gone on to make several trend-setting recordings that illustrate Davis's continuing desire to break new ground in jazz.

The cool, confident trumpet of Miles Davis promises to be a leading force in jazz for many years to come. ∎

Jazz trumpeter Miles Davis founded a new movement in jazz with his album, "The Birth of the Cool."

A Womp Bomp A Loo Bomp

Parents all over America were wringing their hands. "What did we do wrong?" they asked. Senate committees were assigned to look into juvenile delinquency. Something, they said, had to be done about the "youth problem."

Sensational headlines widened the gap between parent and teen. It seemed kids were interested in nothing but this crazy new music called rock 'n' roll. *Other* teen problems parents could handle. They knew firsthand of the danger of alcohol and teen sex. But rock 'n' roll?! This was different. This was something new. Most adults hoped it was just another fad. It would go away, the experts said. Besides, no one could stand all that noise for very long.

Despite what many teenagers think, rock 'n' roll did not begin in 1954. Its roots go back much further. Rock was already cooking in the late 1940s. Negro groups like the Flairs were using the term "rock 'n' roll" long before Elvis Presley was old enough to shave.

But in the mid-fifties, middle-class America caught on to the beat. Bill Haley and the Comets may have been the rock alarm clock that woke up white America. Their "Rock Around the Clock" became a big hit. But not at first. When the record was first released it seemed to drop out of sight. But then it was used in a film called *The Blackboard Jungle*. The movie was about a teacher who

tries to cope with a class of rowdy teenagers. The film became very popular, and Haley's "Rock Around the Clock" did, too.

Bill Haley may have had his comets—but rock 'n' roll had a real *shooting star* in the '50s. His name was Elvis Presley. Presley started out touring the country as "The Hillbilly Cat." But in 1955 he signed a contract with RCA records and quickly became a nationwide sensation.

King of Rock 'n' Roll

In 1956 he recorded "Heartbreak Hotel." It sold a million copies and became a gold record. That same year he had six more big hits. Soon he was being called the "king of rock 'n' roll."

But Presley's style made many adults nervous. They objected to his sexy dancing and swaying hips. They thought he was obscene. When he appeared on some television shows, cameramen were told to film him only above the waist.

If Elvis was too sexy, Buddy Holly was the thinking man's rock 'n' roller. With his horn-rimmed glasses and almost homely looks, he presented a more innocent image. In 1957 he left behind his country western style and recorded a string of rock 'n' roll hits like "Peggy Sue" and "Maybe Baby." Sadly, his career was cut short when he was killed in a plane crash in February 1959.

Other rock 'n' roll singers were more dramatic. Little Richard, a talented songwriter and performer, wore makeup and bizarre clothes. He had a gospel background, and in his music he used gospel's thumping,

Elvis Presley's swaying hips and earthy singing style earned him the title, "King of Rock 'n' Roll."

A WOMP BAM BOOM

rocking rhythms to excite his audience. His "Long Tall Sally" and "Tutti Frutti" went to the top of the charts.

Another important and influential rock 'n' roller was guitarist Chuck Berry. His career has been a rough one. He was disliked by many parents and feared by some in the white community. In 1959 he was arrested in a case that basically sprang from racial tension.

But before Berry's troubles began, he inspired a generation with his songs and his outstanding guitar style. His career took off with "Maybelline" in 1955. Later he had a string of hits that included, "Johnny B. Goode," "Sweet Little Sixteen," and "Roll Over Beethoven."

There were some rock 'n' rollers that seemed to please everyone. Even some parents could not find fault with singers like Ricky Nelson and the Everly Brothers. Their songs were quieter and more innocent.

Once rock 'n' roll exploded on the music scene, its effects could not be undone. Young people everywhere danced and sang along with the beat. More importantly, a youth culture had begun. The Age of Youth was no longer a time spent waiting to become an adult. It was a time of action. It was a time to *rock 'n' roll*! ∎

Chuck Berry wrote some of the best rock 'n' roll tunes of the decade.

The Texan Who Took Moscow

In Moscow they yelled "Vanushka! Vanushka!" In the United States they just called him "Our Van." But no matter what the language, Van Cliburn was the name on everybody's lips in 1958.

The young Texan was the first American ever to win the First Piano Prize at the International Tchaikovsky Competition. His victory in the Soviet-sponsored event was a sweet one. The Soviets had selected 200 of their best pianists to compete. This number was then weeded down to a select group of ten. But Van Cliburn outplayed them all.

For the first time, a classical musician became a popular celebrity. Only 23, Van Cliburn became a kind of international folk hero. He was treated like a movie star or sports figure.

The mayor of New York honored him with a parade. He waved to the cheering crowd as the confetti and ticker tape fell all around him. And his fame was almost as great in Russia. When he met Nikita Khrushchev, the smallish Russian premier, Khrushchev asked him, "Why are you so tall?" The six-foot-four-inch piano player simply replied, "Because I'm from Texas." ∎

He was called "Vanushka" in Russia, "Our Van" in the United States. Whatever the name, concert pianist Van Cliburn is a winner. He won the International Tchaikovsky Competition in Moscow in 1958.

Desi Arnaz seems stunned by yet another of Lucille Ball's plots in "I Love Lucy," one of the highest-rated television shows of the fifties.

America Goes Crazy Over TV

For many years, families have gathered in their homes every night to listen to their radios. They would listen to music, drama, comedy, and news. Then beginning in the early fifties, families gathered in their homes every night to *watch* music, drama, comedy, and news. Americans were fascinated by the latest provider of home entertainment—television.

Television caused quite a controversy during the decade. You either loved it or you hated it. Most Americans loved it. In just five short years, the number of TV sets in U.S. homes jumped from 3 million to 32 million. Soon families were watching about six hours of TV a day.

And what were they watching? The programming ranged from comedy and talk shows to drama and quiz games. Many programs had

their beginnings as radio shows, and they simply carried over to television. "Stop the Music" was one such program. A combination of a music show and a quiz game, it was very popular first as a radio show then as a TV show.

Popular comedians like Jack Benny, Red Skelton, George Burns and Gracie Allen all moved from radio to TV. But many radio performers, convinced that TV was just another fad, lost their careers to "the tube."

Early TV was very different in a special way. Much of it was live. "Your Show of Shows" featured 90 minutes of live television every Saturday night. It starred comedians Sid Caesar and Imogene Coca. A variety show, it combined song, dance, and comedy. It had a regular cast of crazy characters, and famous

guest stars appeared each week. "Your Show of Shows" ran for 160 performances.

Vaudeville Tradition Passed On

Another top favorite was "Texaco Star Theater." Its host and star was "Uncle Miltie," Milton Berle. This show was full of corny gags and slapstick routines. Berle dressed in bizarre costumes. He was a cross between an actor and a circus clown.

Early shows like Berle's grew out of the vaudeville tradition. The style was broad, loud, and very visual. Because TV was live, actors often found themselves in tough spots. For example, when doors wouldn't open or a fellow actor would forget a line, actors had to make do as best they could. Quick thinking and cleverness were very important.

Dramatic productions were as popular as slapstick comedy. This kind of programming was referred to as "serious" television. Each week featured a different play with a different cast. Shows like "Kraft Television Theater," "General Electric Theater," and "Playhouse 90" offered critically-acclaimed dramatic plays.

By the middle of the decade, the face of television was changing. The audience was growing up and demanding more. The old vaudeville style of television was giving way to westerns and more "timely" comedy.

On September 10, 1955, movie star John Wayne came on screen to introduce a new show called "Gunsmoke." Starring a newcomer named James Arness, "Gunsmoke" was the first of many adult westerns that would become widely popular. Others included "Cheyenne," "Have Gun Will Travel," and "Wagon Train." These westerns competed with or replaced earlier, simpler westerns like "The Lone Ranger" and "Hopalong Cassidy."

Perhaps the show that stands out most in the decade is "I Love Lucy." In this zany comedy Lucille Ball played scatterbrained Lucy Ricardo. She was a "typical" housewife who didn't really want to be a typical housewife. In the show she was married to her real-life husband Desi Arnaz, who played Ricky Ricardo, a band leader.

In a typical show, Lucy would try to prove to him that she had great show-biz talent. The action was always the same: she tried to get on stage, and he tried to keep her off. The result was chaos, followed by comic crying fits and eventually a sweet make up. But Lucy never really learned her lesson. The next week she was meddling and scheming again.

The show aired on a weekly basis from 1951 to 1957. In six years it never dropped below third place in the top ten shows.

From the beginning, TV was recognized as a powerful medium. It was praised and condemned, loved and hated. Some called it a drug for the masses. But most people called it wonderful. There's no doubt that TV is here to stay. ■

Some members of the cast of the popular TV Western, "Gunsmoke." From left to right, Milburn Stone, James Arness, and Amanda Blake.

Sid Caesar and Imogene Coca were two of the stars of the weekly variety program, "Your Show of Shows."

Reading on the Rise
Recognizing Literature's Best

Publishers who worried that TV would kill the book business had it all wrong. By the end of the decade, book sales were up by 53%. Americans were reading more than ever.

Publishers wondered if Americans were staying home more. Whatever the reason, there was a huge demand for paperbacks. Reading inexpensive versions of hard-cover best sellers was the rage.

What were people reading? Best sellers included *From Here to Eternity, Doctor Zhivago,* and *Exodus.* But sexy romances like *Peyton Place* and seedy mysteries like *Kiss Me, Deadly* were also big sales winners.

Some authors figured out just what it took to please the ever-growing book-reading public, and that's what they wrote. But others wrote with a higher mission in mind. They wanted to reveal something about human life through their work.

Alfred Nobel wanted to honor such writers. When he died in 1896,

he left a great fortune. In his will he deemed that the money should go to "men and women who have made the most material contribution to the benefit of humanity during the (last) year."

So every year, his "Nobel" prizes are given in categories ranging from literature to physics, and from peace to medicine.

The 1954 prize winner for literature was American Ernest Hemingway. He was given the award for "his powerful mastery of the art of storytelling." The citation read that his skillful writing was "most recently displayed in *The Old Man and the Sea.*"

Hemingway writes crisp, simple prose using very few adjectives or adverbs. His dialogue is often vivid, and his descriptions are clear and exact. He has greatly influenced the style of other American writers.

His Pulitzer-prize winning book, *The Old Man and the Sea* was a dramatic and powerful work. It dealt

with an old fisherman's duel with a huge swordfish in the Atlantic Ocean. It was a tribute to the fighting spirit of man.

A great sportsman himself, Hemingway said, "Man is not made for defeat. A man can be destroyed. But he cannot be defeated."

Hemingway has written several other noteworthy books. They include *The Sun Also Rises, A Farewell to Arms,* and *For Whom the Bell Tolls.*

French Author Cited

Another notable author who won the Nobel literature prize during the fifties was the late Albert Camus. The French novelist and playwright won the award in 1957.

Until winning the prize, he had not been widely read in America. But in Europe he was already highly regarded. Camus was awarded the Nobel prize "for his important literary production."

Highly independent from an early age, Camus was very poor as a boy. He earned money from odd jobs. After attending the University of West Algiers, he became a journalist. During World War II he joined the French resistance fighting the Nazis and edited its underground newspaper, *Combat.*

Camus's books deal with the absurdity of life. But they do not show life as being hopeless. He felt that only if people will *admit* that life is absurd, can they keep their dignity and be free. He has also argued that there are certain things in life worth defending, such as truth, justice, and moderation.

Camus's most famous novels are, *The Stranger, The Plague,* and *The Fall.* His brilliant literary career was tragically cut short when he was killed in a car accident in January 1960. ■

Nobel Prize winner of 1954—Ernest Hemingway.

Jonas Salk
Pioneer in Medical Research

Jonas Salk was responsible for creating a vaccine that has greatly reduced the number of polio victims.

A little girl, age six, starts to cry. She has a headache. Then she develops a fever and becomes nauseous. She lies limp in her bed. She cannot move her legs. Her parents don't know what to do. They encourage her to get up and move around. But no matter how hard she tries, the little girl's body will not obey.

In 1950 there were 33,000 cases similar to this one. Epidemics of these cases have broken out all over the world. A severe outbreak occurred in the United States between 1942 and 1953. And hundreds of other occurrences were reported in Denmark, Germany, Belgium, China, Japan, and the Philippines.

The illness was commonly called "Infantile Paralysis," although the world now knows the disease as polio. No one knows what causes it. But fortunately, someone has discovered how to begin to prevent this terrifying crippling disease.

Jonas Salk, an American physician and scientist, is the medical researcher who is credited with developing a vaccine for polio.

Salk began his research in 1947. In time he identified three separate strains of the polio virus. In the early 1950s he published his finding in the Journal of the American Medical Association. His published work confirmed what other researchers had already suspected.

Salk discovered that a weakened polio virus could stimulate a person's antibodies to fight off a stronger form of the virus. By injecting the weakened virus into a person, the body could then build up an immunity to other stronger forms of the virus. It was a medical breakthrough of enormous significance.

In 1953 Salk announced that he had developed a trial vaccine. Salk gave the vaccine to himself, his wife, and their three sons. It was found to be safe, and there was some evidence that it would be effective in preventing the disease.

The first mass testing occurred in 1954. More than 1,800,000 schoolchildren were injected with Salk's vaccine. By April 1955, the vaccine was pronounced safe and effective.

After Salk's discovery, he received many honors. President Eisenhower presented him with a citation, and he was awarded a congressional gold medal for "great achievement in the field of medicine."

Salk refused any monetary awards for his efforts and returned to his laboratory to improve his vaccine. He hoped that eventually his work would lead to a total victory over the dreaded paralyzing disease—forever. ∎

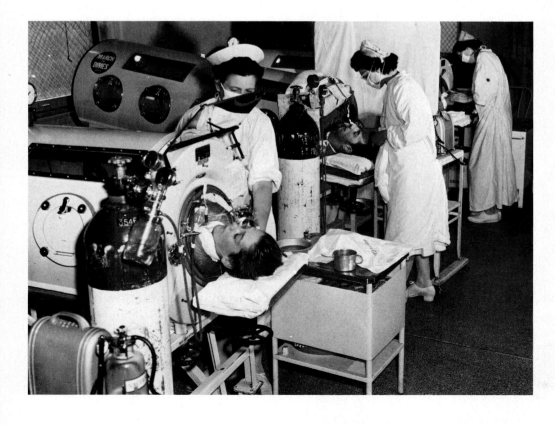

Polio victims were treated with iron lungs and other respiratory devices to help them cope with the paralyzing disease.

The Power Behind Argentina's Throne
Evita Peron

Her name was honored and dragged in the mud. She was loved and hated. She was a symbol of hope for some and of corruption for others. Hundreds of thousands mourned her death. But just a few years later, they destroyed her statues and burned her images.

She was Eva Peron, known as "Evita" to the masses. At one time her autobiography was required reading in the schools of Argentina. After her death, formal requests were made to the pope. Her followers demanded she be made a saint.

Eva Peron had an incredible hold on the people of Argentina. The workers, farmers, and the poor literally worshiped her.

Eva Duarte Peron was born in 1919 in a town outside Buenos Aires. She grew up in a poor family and left home at the age of 15. By 1944 she had become a popular radio actress and was living in Buenos Aires. There she met and married Juan Peron, a colonel in the Argentine army. The marriage changed her life—and the history of her country as well.

In 1943 Juan Peron had taken part in a military coup. By 1946 he had gained enough political power to become president. His power lasted until 1955 when he in turn was forced into exile.

The glamorous Eva was one reason Peron lasted as long as he did. Peron was well aware of her popularity. So he used it to fortify his hold on the government.

In the past, the role of first lady in Argentina had generally been confined to charity work. But Eva Peron was not content with that. She was a strong woman, and she intended to speak out for unions and labor. Many of the Argentine people considered her the "bridge of love" between Peron and the masses. Others said she was just Peron's propaganda tool. But in either case, she was powerful, ambitious, and driven.

Many officers in Peron's government hated and feared her. She did everything she could to make her voice heard. She bought a newspaper. She helped solve a major railway dispute. The people literally demanded, though in vain, that she take the post of vice president.

Eva Peron died of cancer in 1952. Many believe that her death was a major reason that Juan Peron lost his hold on the government and fell from power three years later. Eva, for years the "power behind the throne," was no longer there to help hold him up. ∎

Eva Peron was loved and literally worshiped by hundreds of thousands of Argentineans.

Celebrity, Sex Symbol, Actress
Marilyn Monroe

Marilyn Monroe married prize-winning playwright Arthur Miller in 1956.

For aspiring young movie stars, Hollywood in the fifties was the right time and place. It was also the time and place for gossip about love affairs. Elizabeth Taylor made headlines with her marriage to Mike Todd. Frank Sinatra went from marriage to (and divorce from) Ava Gardner to engagement to (and separation from) Lauren Bacall. And the marriage of actress Grace Kelly to Prince Rainier made her *Princess* Grace of Monaco.

But the reigning queen of American movies, and the star who was most in the news, had to be Marilyn Monroe. Born Norma Jean Mortenson in 1926, Marilyn Monroe had an unhappy childhood. Since her mother was in and out of mental hospitals, she was placed in an orphanage when she was nine years old.

She married a plant worker when she was very young. When the marriage broke up, she threw her energy into becoming a model.

Her hard work paid off. She was offered screen tests and then given a big star build up. Her name was changed to Marilyn Monroe. Soon, her small roles gave way to larger ones. Before long, she was considered Hollywood's hottest rising young actress.

The publication of nude modeling photos both helped and threatened to hurt her career. But she got through that crisis and became even more popular. Films such as *Gentlemen Prefer Blondes, How to Marry a Millionaire,* and *The Seven-Year Itch* made her a star.

In 1954 Monroe married former Yankee slugger, Joe DiMaggio. DiMaggio had been the idol of baseball fans everywhere. Now, he was the *envy* of men everywhere. Many a man dreamed of being married to Marilyn. Her sexy walk, her pouting lips, and her breathy voice excited thousands of American males. However, the Monroe-DiMaggio celebrity "dream" marriage lasted less than a year.

Despite her sex-symbol reputation, Marilyn revealed a desire to play different kinds of movie roles. She wanted parts with greater depth. She went to New York to study acting.

In 1956 she had another highly-publicized marriage—this time to playwright Arthur Miller. When she returned to Hollywood later, she found that she was still in great demand—but for sex-symbol roles.

Marilyn finally proved she could do more than just look pretty. In 1956 she surprised critics with her sensitivity in the film version of the play *Bus Stop.* And she showed sharp comic talent in the 1959 hit movie *Some Like It Hot.* By the end of the decade, Marilyn Monroe had become more than Hollywood's top sex symbol. She was also starting to earn recognition for her acting talent. ∎

Ah . . . School Daze: Everyone knows that America's college students are
supposed to spend long, hard hours either in class or hitting the books at home.
But once-in-a-while they find some time for recreational activities. Here
students from Birmingham-Southern College in Birmingham, Alabama, try a
favorite '50s pastime—phone booth stuffing. These 24 young men set an
unofficial record for the number of people using a booth at the same time.
But . . . can anyone reach for a dime?

The Magnavox Belvedere in stunning blonde oak.

THE BELVEDERE, *with big 20-inch TV, AM-FM radio, 3-speed player. In blonde oak, $610. In rich mahogany finish (illustrated)* **$595** *Available as radio-phonograph only, to which Magnavox TV can be added later; in blonde oak, $350; or mahogany, $335.*

All models readily convertible to Color TV and Ultra High Frequency Channels.

THE WESTOVER. *TV console with 20-inch tube and 12-inch Magnavox speaker. Mahogany finish.* **$35950**

Magnavox . . .

greatest 20-inch television value

Now, every family can afford to own the finest in television.

These new Magnavox 20-inch models are the greatest ever! Finest in sight and sound.

Cabinet styling of heirloom quality in modern or traditional designs.

Yet these instruments are priced way below the market to give this dramatic value.

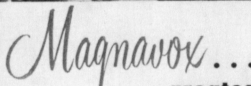

Prices of 20-inch models start at **$35950** *Including Fed. Ex. Tax*

BETTER SIGHT...BETTER SOUND...BETTER BUY

the magnificent

Magnavox

television - radio - phonograph

LOOK FOR THE NAME OF YOUR MAGNAVOX DEALER IN THE CLASSIFIED TELEPHONE DIRECTORY. THE MAGNAVOX COMPANY, FORT WAYNE 4, INDIANA